TIME *after* TIME

A MEMOIR

Susan D. Anderson

authorHOUSE®

AuthorHouse™
1663 Liberty Drive
Bloomington, IN 47403
www.authorhouse.com
Phone: 1-800-839-8640

Published by AuthorHouse 1/14/2013

ISBN: 978-1-4817-0607-0 (sc)
ISBN: 978-1-4817-0608-7 (hc)
ISBN: 978-1-4817-0609-4 (e)

Library of Control Number: 2013900545

Lyrics from "Time After Time" by Cyndi Lauper and Robert Hyman, Dub Notes, Work ID 500357064, ISWC TO702473639

This book is dedicated to Carol Scott Peterson, beloved healer and friend, with profound thanks for sharing the journey to Flying Point and beyond.

Acknowledgements

This is a story about love and rage. Love is easier to deal with: warm, flowing, renewing. Even the most astute, well-balanced adults have a hard time dealing with rage. We need to do something about that, because one of the ongoing tragedies of our society is that some adults are so blinded by rage so much of the time they try to get rid of it by harming a child: sexually, emotionally, physically.

Children who have been the victims of an enraged adult end up either full of rage or full of love. Why such painful circumstances can lead to one extreme or the other is an enigma. But when a profound capacity for loving others emerges from childhood trauma, it becomes metaphysical, transcendent. Sometimes it runs so deep the one-time victim spends a lifetime trying to help others – seeking out people who are suffering, loving those who are needful and hurting. Consider the horrific childhood stories of Maya Angelou, Oprah Winfrey, Tyler Perry and Dave Pelzer in light of the work they have done as adults.

There is something else that we do. We keep reaching back to retrieve the child we once were, to embrace and heal the child who had to endure such torment. That is why the lyrics to the song, "Time After Time," are included at the beginning of this book. Imagine that the words are coming from a healthy, mature adult survivor who is speaking to, honoring, *loving* the child that suffered through that awful situation.

The fact that I emerged from the circumstances described in this memoir as a loving person is owing to the presence in my life of several empathetic and loving people. I am grateful beyond measure for Lorraine Fulton Anderson Delano Melony, who saved me. For my Auntie Belle, who suffered first and poignantly, and who lived to be 90 years old with a feisty independent spirit, the courage to always look forward and an abiding love of God and animals and every hurt person she encountered. For my Uncle Ralph, an inveterate prankster and comic who never forgot. He was my photography teacher, my touchstone and my second father until his death at 91. I am grateful for all the other aunts, uncles, cousins, kinfolk and family friends who knew, and who agonized over their impotence. They were gifted with a sense of humor and a love of laughter. They lovingly insisted on attitude adjustments when I got bogged down in the past. The more I tried to act like them, the happier I became. I am grateful for Grandpa Dan, who tried hard to intervene at an early age, and for Aunt Jessie, who tried again later. For neighbors Millie Ball and Molly Davis, who showed much kindness. For my fourth grade teacher, Mrs. Milliken, who cared.

I am also grateful for my Dad, who was a beautiful person caught in an impossible bind. For Priscilla, who gave me closure in a dream, finally, as I wrote this. In it, she appeared to be living a whole, healthy life in a neighborhood on the spiritual side. She came towards me as I stood in the doorway of my own house, and walked up the front steps to the door I held open. Every inch of her was trim and strong, dressed as Priscilla would dress, pocketbook on her arm, smiling broadly, saying, "I love you," and giving me a smooch on the lips. I'm grateful for Stephen, who tried to be a brother now and then. I forgive you all.

One day I know I will be able to forgive Penny, who went to her grave treating me as Priscilla had taught her I deserved to be treated. For shame, Penny, because you knew better. I hope one day to see you in a dream, letting me know you have read this book and it helped you.

Time After Time

If you're lost you can look – and you will find me
Time after time
If you fall I will catch you – I'll be waiting
Time after time

...Cyndi Lauper/Robert Hyman

Preface

I've spent a lifetime trying to figure out how this story could have happened. The setting is the Boston area, in a time of prosperity. Our post-war nation is feeling the lull of peaceful living. Suburbs sprawl with single-family homes, the ideal location for leisure pursuits and new American dreams of upward mobility. As the baby boom generation arrives, those neighborhoods fill to the rafters with children. Stay-at-home moms occupy lofty pedestals, cloaked in romanticized images of the nuclear family that will last for decades.

Children raised in such advantageous circumstances aren't supposed to suffer. The idea is preposterous. But I have a mother who doesn't try to hide from anyone her bitter and contemptuous feelings towards me; her deep-rooted, utter rejection of my presence in her family. I wish with all my heart to know what it was that set her so solidly against me. I know it had to start when I was still a baby, because that is where my memory begins.

We are out on a fine summer day, going to town for one of our regular sessions with the photographer – Priscilla and her two adorable little girls. As is her custom whenever we go anywhere, Priscilla spent time on our appearance before we left, brushing our hair and dressing us in pretty outfits. She likes it when strangers tell her what beautiful children she has. I am being pushed in the stroller, to all outward appearances a well-tended child, just past my first birthday, my limbs chubby with rolls of baby fat. Fine, blond hair has thickened out enough to surround my head with springy curls. Big sister Penny is almost 4 years old, with pale blue eyes like her mother and her mother's chestnut hair. Anyone can tell she is Priscilla's daughter as she walks beside Priscilla, holding onto the stroller handle.

Suddenly a dog rips through the quiet morning, thundering across a field at us, barking furiously. Penny is screaming, pulling on Priscilla's dress; she's desperate to be picked up and trying to run away all at the same time. In the confusion, the stroller upends. I tumble onto the sidewalk, half tangled in the contraption. In an instant, Priscilla has two crying little girls and a brute of a dog to deal with. It takes a while to sort it all out. Penny's OK but I've been scraped and bruised. One of my fingernails is torn off.

When we finally get home, Priscilla lifts me up to the kitchen counter next to the sink and wordlessly cleans my wounds. When she's done, she wraps a bandage over the injured fingertip saying, "You leave this alone now, do you hear me? It better still be on there when Daddy gets home or you'll get a spanking you won't soon forget. Don't let me see you trying to pick it off. Just leave it alone." Then she abruptly lifts me back down to the floor.

My scrapes and tumbles are usually met with Priscilla's frosty stare and a mean scolding that goes, "Stop that crying. Haven't I told you to look where you're going? It serves you right!" But on this occasion she seems to feel responsible, maybe even remorseful. That little taste of the mothering I long for is so intoxicating! I stand there stock still for a few moments, looking back up at her. Being picked up and held must have jostled primitive remembrances of a time when her maternal gestures were not entirely devoid of fondness. It felt wonderful, delicious. How I relish her touch and wish I could have more! I am desperate to be able to recall that moment later, so that I can draw comfort from it, reliving the human warmth of her body and that hint of concern.

In that instant, memory became an instrument of endurance. I dwelled carefully, deliberately, repetitively on each detail of this event, its proper sequencing, the scenery and background, retelling the story in mental pictures over and over. From the dog to the band aid became the first home movie in my memento box, a jewel I cherished always and contemplated often. Somehow I already knew that those episodes would be rare, knew I needed the memory of a softer moment to help me endure Priscilla's antipathy.

The problem with telling a story of emotional abuse is the apparent insignificance of any one incident when viewed in isolation. "So your mother's mean to you," says the voice of reason. "So what? You live comfortably in a family that is economically stable, providing you with many advantages. A lot of other people in your life care about you. It's like having a bit of muck stuck on the bottom of your shoe. Get over it!" Except one day you realize it's not a little muck; it's the virulent, moldering germ of a crippling disease that will take years to fully manifest. It's not stuck to the bottom of your shoe; it's devouring every particle of your being, until your essential self is beyond recognition. You're witnessing your own disintegration, fragments of who you were meant to be swirling around you, blowing away like dust in the wind.

So that's how the story must be told, in little bits and particles. The early vignettes seem innocuous enough, just a little muck stuck to them. Slowly they accumulate, making pointillist dots on a blank sheet of paper until a picture emerges when you stand far enough away. The focus sharpens from questionable behaviors to deliberately harmful actions. The futility of the situation becomes apparent even as Priscilla's ever more creative manifestations of malice unfold in surprising ways year after year. How can she get away with this? Why doesn't someone stop her?

Hobart Street

Susan, Penny; 1946

Ed, Priscilla; 1946

Family

This is how Priscilla, my mother, talks to me.

"Keep your hands to yourself, Susan."

"Stop your whining."

"Get over here!"

"Stand over there."

"What do you think you're doing? You haven't got the sense you were born with."

"Leave your sister alone. She doesn't need you getting after her every minute of the day."

"I've told you over and over! I shouldn't have to tell you again! Pick up your feet!"

"Serves you right! Haven't I told you time and time again to look where you're going?"

"Put that away."

"Close your mouth, Susan. You look like a moron."

"I'm fed up with you! Sit still!"

"Helpless, hopeless, useless."

"Leave that alone. You've no business with things that don't belong to you."

"How many times do I have to tell you! Pick up your things! Put them where they belong!"

I am a toddler like every other toddler, except the person I have as a mother acts more like the babysitter from hell. It starts when I get up in the morning and continues until I go to bed. It's there when we're alone and it's there when the whole family is together. My mother is always cross with me. The abrupt commands and sharp-tongued scoldings go on day after day. Those are the only times she speaks to me, the only ways she addresses me. On a bus, at the beach, in a store, at a neighbor's house, Priscilla's displeasure with me is part of the experience.

A woman who projects competence and vigor, Priscilla is short, at just over 5 feet tall, with a wide back, substantial arms and legs, breasts that fill her torso. Dark brown hair, curled loosely, falls to her shoulders. Sometimes she wears a ribbon to hold the hair back from her face; it softens her appearance, makes her look more feminine. Pale-as-arctic ice blue eyes have barely a hint of eyebrows and eyelashes. Her nose seems little on a face that has broad, flat cheeks. Her hands also look small, almost delicate with their beautifully trimmed nails. She is graceful with those hands, and dexterous.

Priscilla wears a dress or a skirt and a blouse, always with an apron tied around her waist; the apron stays there all day unless she leaves the house. I used see her in pants when she was doing some gardening, or she'd put on a bathing suit when we went to the beach. Not anymore. "I'm too fat. That stuff doesn't look good on me now," I heard her tell Daddy one day when he was trying to cajole her into wearing some shorts. "I've put it all away for good."

No matter how hot it is or how much floor scrubbing she is going to be doing, she wears a girdle and nylons with the seams in a straight line up the backs of her legs. "Scrwish-scrwish-scriwsh," the nylon-clad thighs say as her feet tap quick steps across the linoleum to the stove. "Scrwish-scrwish-scrwish," as she steps back to the sink.

She goes about her chores in flat shoes, no jewelry or make up. The exceptions are Sundays, or when visitors are coming, or when we are going visiting. Then she dresses up in what she calls her "good clothes" – usually a dress from the women's department at Jordan's or Filene's – gets out her heels, dons a brooch or a necklace, clips on earrings, pencils in her eyebrows and applies a little lipstick.

The signature feature of Priscilla's presence, however, is her ingrained sense of power and superiority. She does not tolerate being challenged or denied, thinks little children should mind their mothers every minute of the day. If she sees me pushing food around my plate without eating anything, or climbing up on the couch, or putting my hand on a curtain as I look out a window, she will stare a hole through my eyeballs without flinching and break my will with a snap of her fingers. The scolding is unnecessary. Her countenance speaks loudly of her displeasures and her disapprovals. A repertoire of gestures – arms akimbo at the apron's waist, the emphatic right toe tap against the floor, the dismissive flip of a hand – telegraph her impatience and her unwillingness to put up with nonsense and distractions, especially from me. She wears her preconceived notions about me the way she wears that apron: as a wall I'll have to penetrate before someone of my filth can have access to a mother. Her demeanor leaves no uncertainty about my inferiority, my mewling weaknesses.

"What are you doing out of your seat? Did I tell you you could get down?"

"How many times do I have to tell you to keep your feet off the furniture?"

"You keep that sweater buttoned up, you hear me?"

"Get your fingers out of your mouth."

"Oh, for Pete's sake. Get a *move* on, Susan. I haven't got all day."

"Haven't I told you not to put your sticky hands on the chairs? Haven't I? Get away from there!"

"I'd like to know how that dress got so wrinkled. You'd think I had nothing better to do all day but wash and iron your clothes! When are you going to learn?!"

If I do something that makes Daddy laugh, right away I look at Priscilla to see if she is laughing, too. Usually she's staring at me with cold eyes, her lips in a straight line. One time I caught her off-guard with the giggles – before she remembered that it was me who did a childishly funny thing and that she doesn't want to ever, ever, ever show that she feels anything but animosity and scorn for me. The minute she saw me looking at her, she wiped all signs of enjoyment from her face. The mask of the anti-mother stared back at me. She needs to make everything about me appear foul.

I can never anticipate what will set Priscilla off. It could be scuff marks on my white toddler shoes, or losing a bow she's put in my hair, or getting crumbs on the floor. One minute she's laughing with Penny or whistling the tune to a song being played on the radio, and out of the blue she catches sight of me, whips around to face me squarely with a pitiless stare and says in the voice of an army training officer barking at new recruits, "I've got better things to do with my time than pick up after you all day. Now get out of the kitchen. I don't need to have you underfoot while I'm trying to get things done."

She is always trying to get things done – on the move, energetic, industrious, the epitome of a suburban homemaker in her early thirties. Priscilla organizes her chores into daily and weekly plans for getting it all done: vacuuming, dusting, washing the kitchen floor, cleaning the bathroom, hanging clothes on the line, cooking, baking, ironing. A talented seamstress, she makes many outfits for my sister and me as well as dresses and aprons for herself. Everything is done to such a high standard a machine could not do better. Her desserts are so beautifully executed they look just like the photographs on the covers of Better Homes and Gardens. She turns out dinners that make Daddy sigh with satisfaction as he sits back in his chair, splays both hands across his tummy and says, "Mummy's a good cook."

Priscilla is indomitable, formidable in every regard. She is so smart and self-disciplined that she completed a two-year course of secretarial studies at Burdett College in 6 months. Before she married, she had been an executive secretary for several years. She is driven to achieve everything to perfection and devotes herself to taking care of her household and her family. Except for me, that is. She wishes I didn't exist.

We live on Hobart Street in Braintree, a suburban neighborhood of modest new 2-bedroom homes for young families, located in Boston's South Shore. My parents, Priscilla and Ed, grew up in the area and have many relatives living nearby. Visits back and forth among our grandparents, in-laws, neighbors and friends are an important part of the family culture.

Today finds Priscilla getting Penny and me dressed in pretty dresses, brushing our hair and taking us on the bus to neighboring Squantum to see her mother, my Grammie. We do this once or twice a week. It's a beautiful day, and as soon as Priscilla gets me out of the stroller at Grammie's house, I run to the steps of the porch, crawl up there with my hands pulling on the next step above, race over to the screen door that Grammie is holding open and run into the house chortling with pleasure at my stair-climbing success.

"Where do you think you're going, young lady?" Grammie says crossly. "Get right back here. Did you wipe your feet? And haven't I told you not to run in my house?" I look up at her as she scolds me for not thinking about her furniture, her polished floor and the grit on my shoes. She is a short, heavyset woman with huge sagging breasts and sagging bags of arm fat, clacking false teeth and a frizzy cloud of sparse gray hair that halos around a bald spot on the back of her head. Her taffeta dress goes practically down to her ankles.

She picks me up and bangs me down on a dark chair in a dark corner of her dining room. "You can stay there until I'm good and ready to let you get down," she says. "You sit still. Do you hear me? Not a move." She takes Priscilla and darling Penny into the kitchen for lemonade and then out to the sunny back yard to admire her many formal gardens overlooking Boston Harbor. A grandfather clock ticks loudly in the silence inside the house. I sit on that chair, alone and quiet, until it's time for Priscilla to put me back in the stroller and head home.

Lucky for me, Grammie and Priscilla are the only meanies in my life. I've got lots of aunts, uncles and neighbors who talk to me with smiles on their faces. They give me hugs and cuddle me on their laps.

Daddy's father takes the bus over on Saturdays from his house in Quincy so that he can visit with Penny and me. Grandpa Daniel has had his share of difficulties in life; now he takes special delight in being a grandfather, spending time with his older son's two little girls while Priscilla feeds him fresh-baked scones and a cuppa tea. However, he doesn't care at all for the way Priscilla shows her fondness for Penny while giving me the cold shoulder. Each time Priscilla packs me off to my crib for things all toddlers do, like touching a magazine on the coffee table after she told me not to touch anything, he voices his dismay. "Bring the bairn back oot noo so I can have ma visit wi' her," he says in his Scottish brogue. "It's been long enow. She's ma wee granddaughter, noo." Grandpa's not afraid to give Priscilla a piece of his mind; he also lectures Daddy regularly.

"It's history repeating itself," he warns my father time after time, referring to the way Grammie dotes on Priscilla, her firstborn daughter, while constantly criticizing and putting down her younger daughter, my Auntie Belle. This practice started in their childhood and continues to this day, in the presence of friends and strangers alike. Grandpa has seen it for himself and heard stories about it from Auntie Belle; they happen to take the same bus into the city every morning.

Grandpa wants Daddy to assert his manly authority and flat out tell Priscilla he will not allow her to be mean to me. Every time they meet for lunch during the work week Grandpa tries to get through to Daddy. "Talk to your wifie," he says. "Put your foot doon. You've got to put a stop to this right noo. Talk to her, Son."

Grandpa's not the only one. Priscilla's overt animosity towards me upsets aunts and uncles on both sides of the family, who try in their own ways to have a word with Daddy about it when they witness her behavior. But they all run into the same brick wall.

Daddy is a devout Christian Scientist.

To the casual acquaintance, Ed appears to be a serene man, given to quietude. He's six feet tall and beefy. His long eyelashes, the ever-present hint of a smile and the deep dimple in his chin give him a sweet face. I've seen him frown once in a while, but he never, ever glowers the way Priscilla does. Once thick and curly dark brown hair is rapidly giving way to baldness; thinning strands cover the top of his head. He looks strong, but when Ed was drafted by the army during WWII he couldn't pass the physical. The idea of flying overseas and fighting in the war so unnerved him he kept hyperventilating and passing out while the doctors were examining him.

Daddy's Christian Science faith is a survival kit for him. His mother, Margaret, died of diabetes when he was thirteen. He got through that trauma by clinging to Christian Science, the church Margaret had joined out of desperation to stay alive in a time when there was no cure for her disease. Grandpa Daniel and my Uncle Ralph, Daddy's brother, continue to experience a great anger at Christian Science for failing Margaret. But Daddy is by nature such a gentle soul he cannot cope with fierce and tangled emotions. His faith calms those stormy seas.

He's also a natural-born stoic. Even when his mother died, he did not, would not cry as a boy. His father has told him all his life that it's not good to hold everything in the way he does. He does not engage in arguments, never raises his voice. However, his mind is rarely at rest. When pushed by his father, his brother or any member of the extended family to confront Priscilla's behavior towards me, he is so busy fixing the facts until they fit his framework of spiritual beliefs he seems to be almost mute, incapable of expressing his thoughts. He's focusing on all the goodness about Priscilla. At most he may utter, "Well. We'll see."

Daddy could no more admit to a flaw in his wife than he could sprout wings and fly. Every day he disciplines his mind to behold everything in life as all perfect. He sees no illness, no mistakes, no harm, no injury. Those things have no reality in a world created by a perfect God who made people in His image and likeness. This is hard work – this having to think your way through to pure good every time you experience something not quite right. He's not so much reticent as he is mentally preoccupied with using Christian Science dogma to perfect his perceptions.

Furthermore, he believes he has chosen the ideal mother for his children. Having experienced childhood with a sickly mother, he has married a woman who is sturdily built, physically strong, emotionally stolid and proficient with the full range of housewife duties. Everyone else calls her Pete, a nickname she's had since childhood. Daddy calls her Honey or Dear, without fail. He starts telling us from an early age what a terrific mother we have.

Three Days in Family Life

A friend of Daddy's was in a parachute troop during the war. Now stationed at nearby Fort Devens, he and his wife have invited us to an air show. His plane is not one of those that will be open to the public for tours, but he will be able to give us special access to it. As we get ready to go, Priscilla tends to Penny while Daddy stands me up on a chair, helps me put on my jacket, and zips it up. Then he carries me and a pillow out to the car, and puts the pillow on the back seat for me to sit on so I can see out the window. All during the ride, Priscilla keeps turning around from the front seat and picking on me.

"Get the hair out of your eyes!"

"I shouldn't have to tell you again! Sit up straight!"

"What's your dress doing up around your waist? Pull it down!"

"Put your legs together!"

"Leave your sister alone! Just keep to yourself the way you've been told time after time."

"Get that hang dog expression off your face!"

"Fold your hands in your lap and sit still for once in your life!"

"Don't bother your father while he's driving!"

We arrive to find Daddy's friend living in air force base housing that is stark and small, like a motel room with a kitchenette. This couple has no children, so adding our family of four to the barren space creates a crowd no matter where we stand. Daddy wants to go out to the tarmac to look at the planes, but Priscilla feels she should stay with our hostess, who is fixing some snacks. "Take *her* with you," Priscilla says crossly, referring to me without looking at me, her arms folded under her breasts. "She'll just get underfoot anyway." Penny stays with Priscilla while I go to the air show with Daddy and his friend.

The planes look monstrous. The cargo planes are immense, of course, but even the sleek fighter jets seem like something out of a book about monsters, with their windowed canopy roofs perched way over our heads, their noses resembling the beaks of giant herons. Daddy holds me tightly in his arms as we navigate around the planes, through the crowds and then over to a section of the airfield that is roped off to prevent the public from wandering around. Grass grows in tufts between cracks in the tarmac. A few metallic behemoths stand there, heads drooping over nose wheels like weary mastodons resting on their tusks. We stop at one that has an open hatch in its underbelly with a ladder positioned down to the tarmac. "Come on," our friend the pilot says, scrambling up the ladder. "I'll give you a private tour inside this old thing."

"Uhh," Daddy says, sweat beads popping out on his brow. He has not been able to overcome acrophobia despite years of applying his Christian Science faith to the problem. He puts a foot tentatively on the bottom rung. "Uhh." I can feel him trembling. The next thing I know he is handing me up the ladder to his friend, saying, "Go ahead, Susan. Take a look inside." He uses his six-foot height to try to stretch his head up high enough to see through the opening. "I'll just look from here."

"NO!" I yell, and start bawling. Not only am I being wrenched from my suddenly nervous father's arms and handed off to someone I barely know, but I am frightened by the dark and cavernous interior of that plane. It's a paratrooper transport; the straps and cords for parachutists are tangled everywhere and seem to go on for miles. The man puts me down on the metal floor, a little bitty child standing in the thick of those snaky things. He says, "Would you like to go up front so you can see where the pilot sits?"

"NO!" I say, wanting only to go back to the daylight and Daddy, who keeps trying with all his might to stretch his head through the opening, repeatedly giving up and mopping his brow with a folded handkerchief, one foot trembling on the bottom rung of the ladder. We are both relieved to get out of that situation.

Ruthie and Charlie, a young couple up the street who have no children, love to dote on Penny and me. We've been at their house overnight while Daddy and Priscilla visit a sick relative in New York. Ruthie lifts me up to her kitchen counter as she is getting breakfast ready and reaches into a cupboard behind me for a small glass.

"Want some orange juice, Sweetie?" she asks,

"I'm not allowed to drink the orange juice at our house," I say.

"Huh? Why not?" Ruthie asks.

"I'm not a good girl," I say. "Mummy says I can't have orange juice until I learn how to behave."

"Now why in the world would she say that?" Ruthie says in exasperation. "You are a good girl, Sweetie. There is no reason in the world why you shouldn't have orange juice, is there, Charlie."

Charlie has been standing behind Ruthie, putting on his necktie, and he reaches around to give me a pat as Ruthie hugs me close.

"We just think you're the best girl in the whole wide world, don't we, Charlie. If you want juice at our house, Sweetie, you can have it," Ruthie says. "I'll never understand why your mother has been treating you the way she does. There's just no reason."

I start to say more about the mean things Priscilla says to me, but just then Penny appears in the doorway from the dining room and we clam up about Priscilla.

"Are you all ready?" Ruthie asks Penny a little curtly, lifting me off the counter, turning her attention to her responsibilities for getting Penny off to Kindergarten. I revel in what I just heard: someone said that Priscilla is wrong and I am a good girl.

An epidemic of whooping cough goes through the elementary school across the street where Penny is in first grade. The Public Health Department puts a "quarantine" sign on many of the houses on our street, including ours.

Grammie comes to visit one day when Penny and I are confined to our beds in the room we share. The door opens and there stand Grammie and Priscilla, side-by-side, built like two stocky peas in a pod, looking in on us. Penny and I, lethargic with the sickness, sit up in our beds to be polite and say hi.

"Here, Dear," Grammie says sweetly to Penny, coming into the room and handing my sister two paper doll cutout books. "You decide which one you want and give the other one to *her*," she says, looking at me as if I am a garden slug. "*She* can't do anything right anyway so it's just going to be wasted on *her*."

Like mother, like daughter. "Are you thirsty, Dear?" Priscilla asks Penny solicitously. "Would you like some juice?" She ignores me, gets Penny her juice, feels Penny's brow, ignores me some more, and leaves.

That's about all the excitement I can take, so I lie back down and sleep for a while. By and by I am lying there, watching Penny as she sits up in bed, cutting out paper doll clothes from one of the new books. I can see that she has already cut out some of the clothes in the other book, too.

"You're supposed to give one to me, remember?" I say. "Grammie told you to give one to me." I feel I must insist, and she reluctantly hands over the other book.

I try to cut around an outfit in the paper doll book so very carefully with my blunt little scissors, making sure to include the little tabs I need to fold the paper outfit over the paper doll, but when I get to the hem of the paper skirt, my scissors get a mind of their own and cut up the middle of it, right up to the waist. Puzzled by the outcome, I start the next one extra carefully, this time choosing a dress. I get up one side, down the other, start to go across the hem, then the scissors suddenly cut the dress right up the middle. I try to cut out a sweater. The same thing happens. And again with a coat. I can't seem to stop this destruction, even though I am aware of what I am doing.

Prince Ave

Penny, Susan, Stephen; 1951

The House and the Home

The old battleship gray Pontiac sedan is parked facing downhill on a side street in Winchester. Daddy and Priscilla left us in the backseat while they went in to look at a house for sale. I'm sitting up on my pillow, feeling tall, looking out the windows at our surroundings on a cloudy spring day.

A boy and a girl walk around the corner and start coming up the sidewalk. Their clothes and faces are covered with dirty streaks. "I guess they don't have jackets," I say to Penny. It's too cold for the short-sleeved shirts they're wearing. Looks like they're a couple of years older than we are.

Oh, goody! They're stopping! I smile at them as they come over to Penny's window, which is open a little. They both have runny noses. Instead of saying, "Hi," like I expect, they start chanting nonsense rhymes and swear words. Penny's too shy to say anything, so I call out, "Don't swear! Swearing is bad."

They start chanting to Penny, "Messy hair. Messy hair." She starts to cry. "Cry baby! Cry baby!" they chant.

"Where's your house?" I ask, wondering if these kids live in the house our parents are looking at.

"Messy hair! Messy hair!" they respond.

"Her hair's not messy!" I tell them. "It's curly! She has curly hair." Penny's hair looks unruly because she's always getting it caught in the open window when she sticks her face up there, trying not to be carsick.

"What's your names?" I ask them.

"Messy hair. Messy hair," the children sing-song, swearing and laughing as they try to poke their filthy faces through the open space in Penny's window. "Cry baby! Cry baby! Messy hair! Messy hair!"

They finally tire of their teasing and move off up the street. Penny continues to cry and is still crying when Priscilla and Daddy come back to the car.

"Why are you crying?" Priscilla asks. Penny is too upset to talk.

"These kids came over and they called her 'messy hair,' and they were dirty and said bad words," I say. "I told them her hair's just curly, but they kept making fun of her."

"Aw, stop your blubbering," Daddy says to Penny. "They're gone now, aren't they? They're not bothering you anymore."

"Pull your dress down, Susan," says Priscilla. "Get the hair out of your eyes. Sit up straight. Mind your own business."

With that bizarre introduction to the neighborhood, the family moves to a three bedroom salt box house in Winchester. We never see the pair of bullying urchins again. This is a peaceful little suburb for Boston commuters, just eight miles from the city and about an hour north of where we've been living in the much more congested town of Braintree. Prince Ave is one of a series of steep hills running in parallel lines down from Highland Ave to the main road below. Our house is the next to the last one at the bottom of the hill. A marshy area cuts through the canted back yard, requiring that we wear rubber shoes all spring.

The neighborhood grocery store sits directly across from the end of our street – a convenience for Priscilla, who doesn't drive. Daddy's train station is only a couple of blocks away. He is moving up the ranks at CH Sprague Coal and Oil, the company he will stay with for the rest of his career. In a few months Priscilla will give birth to their third child. To all outward appearances, our family is just like tens of thousands of others that sociologists will soon lump together with a new label: the upwardly mobile middle class.

For Grandpa Daniel, the move to Winchester marks the end of his visits to our house. "I'll not be going to your hoose again as long as Pete treats that bairn the way she does" he tells Ed sternly over lunch in Boston. "I've tried and tried to get you to put a stop to it; noo, I'm putting my foot doon. You can bring your family to my hoose, but you tell Pete that when she's under my ruif she is not to say a cross word to Susan."

Grammie starts taking the train to Winchester once or twice during the week and staying overnight in the spare room. We're at the breakfast table most Saturday mornings when one of us spots her clumping up the front walk in her heavy shoes with thick heels, wearing her dun colored duster, a stack of boxes from the Mayflower Donut Shop in Boston swinging from her hand. She joins us at the table, passing around the donuts until they're all gone.

This neighborhood is packed end-to-end with young children. We come and go from each other's houses and yards like bees sharing a hive. The mothers are all such nice people! They know all about children and what they need. Their manner is gentle and giving – not just with their own kids, but with any kid who comes through their house. If they are baking, they're apt to say, "Hi, there kids! Want to help me put some frosting on these cupcakes?" Or, "How about a warm slice of bread and butter? I just took a loaf out of the oven." The coffee tables in their living rooms have little dishes of hard candy on them. Anyone can take a piece and eat it, whenever they like, no questions asked. These mothers face you when you're talking to them. They bend down to your eye level, show interest in what you have to say. This is a new generation of relaxed and happy young mothers who wear pants and shorts and drive cars and take kids wherever they want to go.

The kids mill around our yard sometimes. We have speed rolling contests, tumbling from the top to the bottom of the little hill beside the house. We practice cartwheels and jump rope and race our tricycles in the driveway. But the feeling is very different at our house. Priscilla is forever telling us to "keep your voices down," and "stop that racket," and "pipe down out there," because she doesn't want our play to disturb an elderly widow who lives next door.

Our mother gets cranky when kids need to come in for a drink of water or to use the bathroom. "Wipe your feet on the mat," Priscilla says crossly. "You can go right back outside when you're done."

She doesn't like it when Penny or I come inside for something and a pile of kids comes through the door with us. "Oh, for goodness sake!" she mutters. "What do you want? Why do you all have to come in? Can't one of you just come to the door?"

Penny becomes best friends with a girl her age that lives across the street from us. This family has the first television on the block. All of the kids in the neighborhood go over before supper to crowd around the little black and white screen and watch the Howdy Doody Show and the Pinky Lee Show. While all the other mothers are busy in their kitchens getting dinner ready, this neighborhood mom is just as busy, but she doesn't mind at all having a dozen or so kids sitting around her living room watching TV. She's happy that her child has friends; that's what's important.

Daddy comes home right about when the shows end, and Penny and I pester him about getting a TV of our own someday. "Sure," he says. "We'll get six of them – one for every room!" That's what he always says when he thinks something is too expensive.

It's not just the enjoyment of watching TV programs we're after, however. My sister and I, having had a chance to come and go from so many neighborhood households, share a new, unspoken longing to have the kind of mother who would be happy to let a bunch of kids come into our living room every day just to spend an hour giggling together at the antics of the clowns on the screen. But Priscilla is not like that. Her girls are expected to conform to the needs of their parents, not the other way around.

So when Daddy calls us in from our play one Saturday and says, with all the excitement and pride of being a good father, "Look what we have!" pointing to the big TV console that now sits in our living room, our reaction catches him off guard.

"Oh. A TV," Penny and I say, and rush back outside to play with the kids.

My best friend is Hope, who lives in the house behind ours on the next street over. Being in Hope's house is always an adventure: it's a 3-story Victorian, with hidden stairways, nooks and window seats in the bowed corners. She has younger sisters named Faith, Patience, and Prudence. We take turns giving them rides on the swings or pulling them up and down the sidewalks in a wagon. We hide from them, too, although I think it's pretty neat that Hope has real babies to play with.

The two of us especially like to play with Paul, who lives next door to her, and with Richard, who lives up the street from me, near the top of the hill. We'll all be in the same Kindergarten class in September, which is very exciting. I will be able then to get out of Priscilla's world every day and spend time with my friends.

Penny and I have each been given a brown paper bag full of cloth scraps from the sewing projects that Priscilla and Grammie have underway all the time. The bags have an assortment of buttons, needles and pins as well. The idea is that we can use all this to make doll clothes. I like to spread an old blanket under the tree out back or on the living room floor so I can dump out the whole bag, look at all the different colors and textures and see what might be made into something for my dolls.

There's an obstacle, though. Penny is getting sewing and knitting lessons from both Grammie and Priscilla, neither one of whom would spend two minutes with me teaching me anything, no matter how sweetly I asked. Knitting appeals to me, the idea of watching a colorful scarf or a mitten slowly emerge from what was just a ball of yarn. "Can you teach me to knit?" I ask Penny. She hesitates. "Well, I don't have needles and yarn for you," she says. "You'd have to get that from Mummy." Something in her wants to help but feels caught. "If Mummy and Grammie aren't teaching you, I don't think I can."

Mostly Penny observes my outcast treatment without comment or facial expression. Once in a while her attitude towards me mimics

Priscilla's, like the other day when she scoffed at my efforts to sew a skirt for my doll. "That's not how you do it!" she said with her superior nose in the air as she walked by.

We play together down cellar on rainy days, staying out of Priscilla's way. There's a fireplace down there where Daddy lets us cook hot dogs and marshmallows on rainy weekends, like we're camping out. When Daddy's not around, we pretend we're having a cookout with our dolls. There's an old fashioned baby pram in the cellar, and a purple velvet chaise lounge of Grammie's, stuffed with horsehair that rustles whenever you move.

For the most part, though, Penny has started to go her own way, as if I am of no importance to her. She plays with me at a distance, doesn't get too involved, keeps off to one side a lot, doing her own thing. If Grammie and Priscilla aren't helping me to learn cooking and sewing and knitting, if they can't be bothered taking time for me, I guess she figures I'm not worth her efforts either.

And why should I be? Priscilla has set up our sister relationship such that we have to play our assigned roles: one sister is good and one is bad. One has to be treated as a darling, a paragon of virtue and perfection, the apple of her mother and father's eye. Everything Penny does is wonderful and beautiful. Penny does things right and to her mother's satisfaction. Penny is helpful. Penny is smart. Penny is the ideal daughter. I am treated as an onerous and defective imposition in this family, an imbecile, someone who has no worth and does nothing of value. The arrangement guarantees that only one of us will be fully entitled to mothering and affection under all conceivable circumstances. Two would be too many. At least it seems like that's the big idea behind all this.

Penny's role is not so easy, either. She's a quiet, serious girl, even when we're playing outside with a group of kids. Priscilla calls her "Dear," listens to everything she has to say, responds to her with affection and interest. But Penny has to do everything just right all the time so that Priscilla doesn't have a chance to scold her or treat her the way she treats me. At least, that's what I imagine it must be like to be Penny. She seems almost adult-like to me, a seven-year-old Priscilla. She's more grown up than other children her age. But there's a chronic, runny rash on her arms, she gets sick every ten minutes whenever we go anywhere in the car and the only friend she seems to have is the girl across the street.

Priscilla's meanness is getting worse and worse. She bullies me constantly.

"What's that sock doing under your bed? There's no excuse for this! Where does it go? Huh? What have you got to say for yourself, huh? What have I told you time and time again to do with your dirty clothes?"

"Just look at the toothpaste all over this sink! Haven't I told you time after time to clean up after yourself? There's no excuse for this! Now get in here and clean that up!"

"Is that how you're supposed to fold the towel when you're done? Don't be such an imbecile. Do it the way you've been taught."

"Just look at the mess in this drawer! Why haven't you put your things away the way I told you to? There's no excuse for this! I shouldn't have to tell you time after time. You haven't got the sense you were born with!"

"What have you done? Broken another barrette? It's just another example of your carelessness. Helpless, hopeless, useless. I suppose you think your father's made of money! What have you got to say for yourself, huh? You'd better start taking care of your things or you'll get a spanking you won't soon forget!"

I have no defense for these attacks. I'm too scared to speak, and too worried that whatever I say will get me in more trouble.

Priscilla puts meals on my plate, washes and irons my clothes, brushes my hair and makes my bed. But her "mothering" of me is as devoid of physical contact as she can get it. She lets me know how put-upon she feels to have to do anything for someone who "doesn't mind her mother," and "doesn't lift a finger to help out round here," and "just takes, takes, takes." So many things remind her that I am a blood-sucking parasite: a rip in my jeans, a lost button, a hole in my socks, a drippy nose, long fingernails, outgrown shoes, having a birthday. She would like to ignore me but I keep on being there, in the house, a young child in need of things. She's cast herself in the role of some beleaguered maid who provides my incessant basic care – food, clothing, shelter – solely because she's unable to get out of doing that much for me. As far as she's concerned, I don't belong in her family.

She continues to speak to me only when she wants to scold me or criticize me. She does not want me to speak to her at all. I act as if we can have conversations, but she interrupts me when I try to talk to her about one of the kids or what we've been doing. "I don't care," she says flatly. "I'm not interested in anything you do."

Just asking if I can go to a friend's house has become an ordeal. I have to practice phrasing it right in my head. "Please may I go over to Paul's house to play?" If I don't say it right she won't even answer me.

A lot of times I don't bother asking for what I want, because it's not worth it to get the lecture I'm going to get about not having done anything to earn the right to go anywhere, do anything or have anything. Then there's the alternative speech that goes, "I'm busy. I don't have time for your selfishness." She gets revved up and starts yelling. "When have you ever done anything for me? When was the last time you offered to do something around here? Now get out of here." It sounds like it's about her, about my inability to take care of her needs. She has no investment in me and no concern for my well-being.

I search Priscilla's face all the time, hoping that the more I look the better my chances of catching a glimmer of affection for me, even though she gives no hint of that. I'm desperate for her approval, yet so ashamed of being an unloved child that I don't want my friends to see how she treats me. I love her fiercely, against all odds. I need a mother. Solely because she is my mother, I want her to see my love and love me back. I keep trying to think of ways to woo her, things to say and do to make her love me.

But I don't want to be near her because she will find fault with me the minute she sees me, no matter what. I'm afraid of her because she physically hurts me without warning by pulling my hair, spanking me or yanking me roughly by the arm. Otherwise, she doesn't touch me if she can avoid it, and when she needs to touch me for the sake of brushing my hair or adjusting my clothes, her touch is rough. She can't wait to be done.

"Get out of my sight," is what she says. "I have no use for you."

Upward Immobility

Daddy is getting ready to go to the dump. First he backs the car out of the garage, then he turns it around so it's facing out of the driveway. He pulls the red metal trailer into position, hitches it onto the car's bumper and opens the back gate on it. One by one he heaves the trash barrels inside.

Penny is getting ready for the dump, too. She takes the old newspapers that have been stacked up in the cellar and ties them into bundles with string. When she's done, she carries those out to the trailer for Daddy to heave in. I climb into the back seat for the ride over, already turning green with envy.

At the dump, a man weighs the newspaper bundles and gives Penny a dime for them. Penny gets to keep the dime. It's her allowance. She has spending money; I don't. The inequity of being the unloved daughter is enough without having to be the penniless one as well.

The issue of money probably shouldn't concern a four-year-old, but I have my reasons. First, there are the gift cards. Every time a holiday or birthday comes up, Penny takes her savings to Woolworth's and picks out the cards she wants to give each person. I have to get money from Daddy, and he limits me to what he thinks is a proper amount for a little girl, which is usually a nickel a piece. The cards I'm drawn to always seem to cost too much. I want pretty cards with ribbons and lace, full of loving sentiments, showing these people what a sweet person I really am.

Second, Penny has been buying materials and making gifts: a woven pot holder, a hankie, a bookmark. The adults in our life admire this trait — someone who can make her own gifts, products of her own labors with knitting and sewing. I can only think up gifts for which the bottom line is money I do not have. Penny's gifts are cherished; mine are pathetic, plastic acts of desperation from the five and dime.

On the way home I get to ride in the trailer. It's so bumpy back there! I have to hold onto the side sometimes or I get tossed around. But I love peeking over the rim as we ride along, seeing so much at once, feeling all that wind in my face. Penny used to ride back here with me, but it made her feel sick so she sits in the front seat now with Daddy. As much as I love dump day and riding in the trailer, every time we head home my lack of income looms over me like a storm cloud over a picnic. I'm forever scheming of ways to make some pocket change.

We get back and Daddy unloads the empty trash barrels from the trailer. Standing off to the side of the driveway as he works, I try out my newest money-making idea on him. I sing to him all the verses of "Oh My Papa."

Oh, my pa-pa, to me he was so wonderful
Oh, my pa-pa, to me he was so good
No one could be, so gentle and so lovable
Oh, my pa-pa, he always understood.

That song, written and sung by Eddie Fisher, plays constantly on the radio Priscilla keeps on in the kitchen as she goes about her cooking and cleaning. She listens to the Arthur Godfrey show, Dave Maynard and the rest of the WBZ weekday programs. In a flash of insight one day, I suddenly understood what a song is: the music is always the same, the words stay the same, and you can learn it and sing it yourself.

"Very good," Daddy says. "Where did you learn that?"

"I heard it on the radio," I say. "Do you think anyone would give me a nickel to sing it to them?"

"No," Daddy says as he fastens the trailer's gate with a clang. "I don't think so. They can just listen to it on the radio."

Richard is having a birthday party with pony rides! All the kids are talking about it. When my invitation comes Priscilla says she doesn't see any reason why I should go, since I can't even mind my mother. "Where are you going to get a present to bring?" she taunts me. "You just expect us to go out and buy something? Why should we spend your father's hard-earned money on you?" I am in a state of nervous anticipation for days, trying so hard to be good enough for Priscilla to let me go and afraid there's no chance.

The hot and humid morning of party day, my long hair is done up in braids encircling my head. I have been careful to keep it in place while I stay quiet and out of Priscilla's sight. Finally Priscilla calls me inside. She and Grammie are upstairs in the spare room where Grammie sleeps when she stays over. They are knitting baby's clothes.

"Go take a bath before you get dressed," Priscilla orders, and I race to my room to undress, knowing that means I can go to the party. One of my sundresses is lying across my bed, all nicely ironed. It's not the sundress I like the best, but I won't say a word. I go into the bathroom and notice that the tub is empty.

"There's no water in the tub," I call out to her.

"Oh for goodness sake." Priscilla splutters from across the hall. "You're old enough to run your own bath. I don't see why I should wait on you hand and foot."

I've never filled the tub myself, so I have to think about this a little. I put the rubber plug in the drain, turn on the faucet, and let the water run. Pretty soon Priscilla calls out in her harshest tone, "That's enough! There's no need to waste your father's hard-earned money." I turn the water off. I step in. And then I scream.

"Now what's the matter," Priscilla says angrily, lumbering into the bathroom as if she's weighted down with a sack of cement in her tummy. She's dressed in a white top as big as a tent, with decorative eyelets and red piping on the collar and sleeves. It nearly covers her skirt. For once the apron is missing.

"It's too hot!" I cry. I didn't know you had to mix hot and cold. I had only turned on the hot water faucet. The water is scalding. Now Priscilla is really in a tizzy, scolding me for all the extra work I cause her and ranting that I need to stop acting like a baby and I should know how to run my own bath water by now instead of expecting my mother to do everything for me.

"You haven't got the sense you were born with. Get in there!" she says angrily after adjusting the water. "And get yourself cleaned up! If you don't hurry up you're going to be late! Helpless, hopeless, useless."

By the time I finish with the bath ordeal, put on my sundress with the complicated criss-cross straps, and stand on the little stool to brush my teeth, I am so wound up I wet my pants. Priscilla has to clean me up and change me into a different sundress, this time choosing the one I really like. She helps me to get myself back together, slaps a wrapped present in my hand to bring to Richard (I've no idea what it is), and sends me on my way.

The bedtime ritual for Penny and me has been the same for as long as I can remember. We go upstairs, get undressed, put on our nighties, stand on the little stool by the bathroom sink to brush our teeth, then go back downstairs to the living room to kiss Priscilla and Daddy goodnight. Priscilla follows us back upstairs to "tuck us in." That means she pulls down the window shades, helps Penny say her prayers, ignores me while I say mine, fusses over Penny's sheets and blankets, kisses Penny on the brow, and says to Penny, "Good night, Dear. Sleep tight." She doesn't look at me, touch me, or address me unless she has something to scold me about.

One night, as our first summer on Prince Ave is coming to a close and the school year is fast approaching, Penny and I tumble down the stairs and into the living room to kiss our parents good night. Priscilla is on the couch, as usual, doing some knitting. Daddy is in his easy chair, as usual, reading a Christian Science Quarterly from the stack on the floor. As I wait my turn, Penny kisses Priscilla on the cheek, then goes over to Daddy. I lean in as usual to kiss Priscilla's cheek. She jerks her head away. "I don't want any kiss from you," she says coldly. "Until you can learn to mind me, it doesn't mean anything to me." Her tone is as harsh as if she is the owner of an animal shelter and I am an intruder caught strangling baby bunnies.

I am stunned, paralyzed. What did I do today? I have no memory of anything specific that would cause this drastic reaction. I am just me: a five-year-old little girl, dressed in a nightie, her favorite doll tucked under her arm, coming to say good night to her mother and father. I look over at Daddy, who seems oblivious, deep into his Christian Science article. He is not looking, not responding to this, not offering any help or condolences for the beating my feelings are taking. The room starts to shrink down. I see black shadows all around me. "Good night, Mummy," I say softly, then go over to kiss Daddy's check. "Good night, Daddy." He gives me a kiss, says good night, doesn't turn away.

After Priscilla has tucked Penny in and shut the door, I lie awake for a long time. My age of innocence is over. I know with a cruel certainty the life I am going to be living. Realities march into my consciousness, like soldiers breaking through torn membranes that had been preserving the last remnants of my childish naiveté.

My mother does NOT love me.

Not at all.

Not even a little bit.

She never will love me.

She is going to keep thinking up ways to be mean to me.

There isn't anything about me that she likes.

She hates me.

Harsh, truth-telling sentences keep on forming, one after the other, piling up. A line that divides time has been drawn. Before, I went from one event to the next, one day to the next. Now I see the whole. Now I am stuck with the reality that has finally penetrated my foolish brain.

It doesn't matter what I do.

Susan D. Anderson

It doesn't matter how I behave.

I could be perfect and she'd still hate the sight of me.

She is going to find fault with me no matter what.

No one in the family will come to my rescue.

Daddy will never see anything wrong with the way Priscilla treats me.

Penny doesn't want to help me and will only get in trouble if she tries.

There is no one around who can help me.

I am all alone. I am totally alone. I am so very, very alone.

I dwell on each thought, over and over, making myself see the truth until I finally understand that there is no hope. The situation is not going to get better, only worse. It won't matter how hard I try to be the good girl Priscilla says I need to be. I am going to have to endure this treatment on my own, every day, all the time, no matter what I do.

I am never going to have a mother who loves me.

I will always be an unloved child, someone who doesn't belong in this family.

No one else I know has to deal with this. I am a freak.

I think about the years remaining. How old do I have to be before I can leave? Eighteen? I count it out: thirteen more years before I am eighteen. I haven't even started school yet. Thirteen more years before I can walk away from Priscilla. In my mind I can see those years stretching from now into eternity. I'll never make it. I can't possibly live this way every day for all that time. Running away is the only out. I have got to get some money. If I don't have money, I can't go anywhere.

I lie awake for a long time, considering these facts. That leads to trying to figure out what to do about the good night kiss from here on. Seems like I should just skip her and kiss Daddy good night. But then, if I don't try to kiss Priscilla's cheek, if I avoid her, it will look like I'm deliberately ignoring my mother. I'll be soundly scolded for not appreciating her and all the hard work she does to take care of me. I decide I have to approach her every night as if the kiss on the cheek might be allowed. And every night, year after year, she snaps her head away.

The Frightful Fives

Penny and I have been staying in beautiful, ocean-hugging Marblehead with Bob and Hope, Daddy's Christian Science friends. They are sweet people who treat us lovingly and manage to distract us from wondering why we're here and when we'll go home. Maybe Penny knows, but I don't. Finally they drive us back to Winchester, where there is a surprise waiting: Priscilla has a tiny baby in her arms. Now that makes sense of everything! I've heard those stories about storks delivering babies to their designated families.

His name is Stephen. He's really cute, with dark hair like the others in the family, and wide open eyes; they're a soft pastel blue like Daddy's. In a couple of months I will be allowed to pose with him in my arms so that Daddy can take a picture. Until then, I get used to the bassinet tucked in a corner of the kitchen, the baby bottles in the sink and Priscilla's face covered by a gauze mask when she's changing his diapers.

This is all very exciting because now I have a chance to study what happens in infancy, the part of my own life I can't remember. What do babies do? Could there be a fatal mistake some babies make that turns their mothers against them? How does Priscilla respond to a baby? He's the only boy; I know that's to his advantage. Too bad Stephen doesn't have light hair like me. Will Priscilla treat him the way she treats Penny, or the way she treats me? What will he do that will tip the scales one way or the other? My curiosity about Stephen's fate is immense.

He sleeps. He rarely cries, and always looks content in his baby blue clothes that Priscilla and Grammie crochet, swaddled in blue blankets they sew. He has a padded red plaid carrier that sits on the floor of the back seat of the car whenever we go on visits. As we make the rounds of relatives and friends, Priscilla and Daddy tell everyone what a big baby Stephen was at birth: "Almost 10 pounds!" They describe him to one and all as "a good baby." The visits and hours of backseat observation roll by. I never even see him squirm. No matter how long a drive lasts, he sleeps through it every time. Priscilla is very happy with my brother.

"You stay away from the baby, you hear me?" Priscilla says crossly, time after time, like I'm a poltergeist who wants to turn her beautiful baby boy into a little demon. "I've got enough to do without having you interfering all the time," she says. Sometimes, when she's hanging clothes on the line or cooking in the kitchen, I ask her if I can watch him for her, like Penny does, but she says, "I don't need any help from the likes of you." Slowly I come to understand that to be a good girl I will have to hold myself in the margins of this experience. It's wiser to rein in my interest in Stephen so that I don't cross some invisible line Priscilla is drawing around my role in the family.

I am willing to do even that to earn some regard from her, but it doesn't do me any good. "Penny is so helpful with the baby," Priscilla tells all who will listen. Then with a cold look in my direction, "*That One* doesn't lift a finger to help out."

The first time I heard this, my sense of moral outrage was born. I nearly blurted out in protest, "But you keep telling me to stay away from him!" Talking back to your mother, however, is strictly forbidden.

The first day of Kindergarten is finally here! I have new skirts, blouses, dresses, slips, underwear, socks and shoes. Some of my clothes are hand-me-downs from Penny, although she is built like Priscilla so most of her clothes are too big for me. Priscilla made some of my dresses, and some are from the store. My favorite dress is navy blue with a white collar and red cherries embroidered on the front. From now on, certain outfits belong to a category of "school clothes," which are too good for play and not good enough to wear to Sunday School, which I will also be starting to attend.

Last week Daddy bought pencil boxes for Penny and me at his favorite stationery store in Boston. Mine has two fat red pencils, a pencil sharpener, a ruler and an eraser, each nestled it its own compartment. The lid has a snap to keep it closed. I've had a hard time keeping my hands off of it as I try to imagine what it will be like to sharpen the pencils and keep the box inside a desk of my very own. All the kids will have pencil boxes this morning, and I will walk with them and go to school. I can't wait! Now I have an excuse to be out of the house and with my friends for a whole morning, rain or shine, day after day. I won't have to ask permission.

"Penny and Susan. Come here and say good-bye to your father," Priscilla says after breakfast. She and Daddy are standing in the front hallway, anticipating their ritual good-bye kiss as he puts on his hat and gets ready to walk to the train station. They both inspect the way I've dressed myself in a rust-colored dress Priscilla made for me, the one with yellow rick-rack around the collar and the cuffs.

"Bye, Daddy," I say.

"You've got your pencil box?" he says, seeing it clutched in my hand.

"I've got it," I say, holding it out.

I expect him to say, "Have a good day!" or "Don't take any wooden nickels!" but instead he says, grinning, "Don't put any marbles up your nose!"

My first day of Kindergarten ends abruptly when the principal gives me a ride home in the middle of the morning. I have to lie still on the couch in the living room until the doctor comes. He probes with a flashlight and rubber tweezers to remove the marble I stuck up my nose. Only a bad girl would cause all that trouble.

Penny and I are standing in the front hallway with suitcases in our hands. Priscilla is inspecting us carefully and issuing instructions. "Mind your manners, you two. Do what the adults tell you to do. Remember you're a guest in that house." Penny is going to stay with her friend across the street for a couple of days; I am going to stay with Paul's family. We've already had lots of practice sleeping at other people's houses whenever our parents are coping with some emergency that they feel children have no business knowing about, but Stephen is a tiny baby and will have to stay with Priscilla and Daddy.

This time it is the unexpected death of Grandpa Daniel. He came home early from work complaining of a severe headache, went to bed, and immediately died of a brain hemorrhage. Just the day before, Priscilla's father, Grandpa John, was hospitalized with a stroke. Now she and Daddy have to shuttle back and forth between the arrangements for Grandpa Daniel's funeral services and bedside visits with Grandpa John in the hospital.

Two days after Grandpa Daniel's funeral Penny and I are standing once again, in the front hallway, being inspected, with suitcases by our side. Grandpa John has died. "Mind your manners, you two," Priscilla says again. "Do what the adults tell you to do. Remember you're a guest in that house." Penny is going back to her friend's house across the street. I am going to stay with Richard this time.

When Priscilla tells me that, she says, "You're just too much trouble to have the same people take you both times." The real story is that she hasn't bothered to develop relationships with the mothers of my friends. "I'm not interested in anything that has to do with you," she'll say flatly when I try to tell her something about neighborhood families and houses and goings-on. "When you can bother to behave yourself, maybe I'll bother to listen." I'm being shunted off on a different family this time because it doesn't feel right to Priscilla to ask the same little-known neighbor for this big favor twice in one week.

"You girls remember everything your father and I have taught you," Priscilla says, her voice subdued. "Be on your best behavior and mind when people tell you to do something." She's lost her usual sharp edge with me, having far too much else to cope with this week. She's even kneeling down to fix my barrette one last time. She never kneels down to tend to me at eye level. That's why I am going to remember the moment.

I am old enough to do some chores. On Saturdays, I use the dustpan and brush to clean the cellar stairs – one by one, descending on my knees. Afterwards, Priscilla inspects the stairs to make sure I get all the corners and don't leave a speck of dirt. You'd think a grain of grit was a mountain of rocks the way she belittles me for missing something, so I try really hard to brush them clean.

Before Penny or I can leave the table after each meal, we are required to chant, "Excuse me from the table and thank you for my (breakfast), Mother Dear." Daddy must have thought that one up. Technically, this is not a chore; it's a silly little ritual. But it feels like a chore. I could choke on that "Mother, Dear" phrase. It's my job to clear the dishes from the table after each meal and bring them out to the kitchen counter by the sink. "Excuse me from the table and thank you for my breakfast/lunch/dinner, Mother Dear," I recite as I begin.

Our everyday dishes are yellow Melmac, lightweight and unbreakable, but Priscilla scolds me harshly if I drop something or make too much of a clatter. "Oh, for Pete's sake. Don't you ever pay attention to what you're doing? You're old enough to do things the way you've been told to do them. I shouldn't have to get after you at this stage of the game. Hurry up now. There's no need to take all day."

I can't get away with forgetting to take something away, either. The sight of a dirty spoon or used napkin left behind on the table sends Priscilla into a rant about my incompetence that always includes, "Why can't you do anything right?" and ends with, "Helpless, hopeless, useless." On Sundays, after the big midday dinner, I don't have to clear the table because that's when we use the good china dishes. Lots of times company comes on Sunday afternoons for coffee and dessert; they get the good china, too.

I polish my shoes on Saturdays, both the school shoes and the Sunday shoes. If I'm sloppy or careless, the polish rubs off on my socks and Priscilla gets mad about that. "I'm not going to clean up after your messes time and time again! Now do it the way your father taught you to do it. Helpless, hopeless, useless."

The nickel I get for these chores is given to me on Sunday mornings, just before we leave for church, and has to be used for the Sunday School collection. Priscilla says, "Your father and I are not about to give you money when you have to be made to do a few things around here. When you start making an effort to help out the way your sister does, then we'll see about an allowance."

I like going to Sunday School because I ride in the front seat of the car right next to Daddy. Penny sits by the window in the front seat and I am in the middle, protected; no Priscilla. She stays home to cook the Sunday dinner and take care of Stephen. She doesn't want anything to do with Christian Science. As Daddy drives, he is always snaking his hand over to tweak one of the long hairs on my leg, grinning and saying, "Gotcha!" His affectionate attention makes me happy. For the span of two ten-minute Sunday drives, going to church and coming home, I feel like a normal kid.

I wake up with a miserable sore throat, in the children's ward of the hospital. Several white beds with railings line the walls around the room. The other kids are crying for their mothers. Every single one of them. A nurse says to them, "Look at Susan over there. See what a good girl she is? She never cries for her Mommy." If she only knew.

I've had my tonsils out. Apparently I've been prone to colds and nasty coughs. My Christian Scientist father has agreed to this medical solution because he defers to Priscilla whenever the issue concerns her health or the health of one of the children.

Daddy can't bear the thought of the hospital, and Priscilla would just as soon I didn't exist, so a couple of days go by before I see them. I watch the other kids' parents hover over them every minute they're allowed to visit – laughing, bringing presents, helping their children back to wellness. I watch mothers lovingly wrap their sons in favorite blankets and I watch fathers pick up their daughters in strong arms to carry them home.

When my parents finally come for a visit, they stand at the foot of my iron crib like an old world couple who don't know English and understand little of what is going on. They are bundled up in their winter coats. Daddy holds his hat in his hand; Priscilla holds her purse by its handle. Their awkwardness standing there is palpable. There's no touching and fussing over me the way parents do, the way these same parents would if it were Penny or Stephen in the crib. Because it's me, the child Priscilla can't stand, they don't know what to say or do.

"The doctor gave me a nickel," I tell them, "but I lost it." My voice sounds funny, and it hurts to talk.

"Of course," says Priscilla. "Careless as usual. It's your own fault, isn't it. You haven't done anything to deserve any money anyway."

"I hid it under my pillow and now it's gone," I manage to rasp out, trying to defend myself against her typical accusation. I needn't have bothered. That stone face has its lips set in a thin line. That mind is made up about my character: I am worthless through and through, undeserving of a shred of her regard even when I've just had an operation and am lying in a crib in a hospital.

They leave within minutes of their arrival. Daddy can't seem to muster enough parental gumption to come 'round to the head of the bed and give me a reassuring pat or something. He just wants to get out of there.

At home a couple of days later, I am placed on the couch in the living room with pillows and blankets. My coloring books and crayons are on the coffee table right by the couch. Priscilla comes in from the kitchen and says, "Sit up!" with a snap of her fingers. She places a large crockery bowl full of warm tapioca pudding in my lap and gives me a spoon. The offering looks like it has little glass pebbles in it. "Eat that," she says, "and don't let me hear you whining for anything else. I haven't got time to cater to you every time I turn around."

She leaves. The tapioca is lovely, warm and sweet. "She made this especially for me," I think, as the first spoonfulls slide down my sore throat. "That's worth remembering." For the rest of the day Priscilla stays busy in the kitchen. Once in a while I hear her going through the dining room and up the stairs. I am left alone. No conversation; not a glimpse of her or of Stephen. I might as well be a piece of furniture. The remains of the pudding slowly congeal. I nap a lot.

Just before suppertime, the mother across the street comes over for a visit. Priscilla quickly removes the half-eaten bowl of gelatinous pudding, grabs two straight-backed chairs and pulls them right up to the couch. "Oh sure. She's right here. She's been napping for a while." She acts all solicitous, fussing with my blankets, plumping the pillows, straightening the crayons. As if she's been right by my side all day!

"So the operation went well?" the neighbor asks. "I was worried when I didn't see Susan come home for a few days."

"Oh, no," Priscilla says. "It went fine. They said she was very good about it."

"She's such a good girl," the neighbor says. "I brought you something, Susan." She shows me a plastic Santa Claus with lollipops sticking out of his sack and puts it down on the coffee table. "Lollipops taste pretty good when you've got a sore throat. Are you feeling a little better today? I've been looking forward to seeing you back home."

She turns to Priscilla. "You must be very proud of her. Look at her, lying there so quietly, not making any fuss at all. She's a real trouper."

"Oh, ya," Priscilla agrees. "She's done very well with this. The doctor timed it so she wouldn't miss much school, with Christmas vacation next week. She just needs to stay quiet like this for a few more days."

It's obvious that Priscilla feels under some obligation to come across as a concerned mother. Faced with a pushy neighbor who is making it clear that a five-year-old's tonsillectomy deserves special attention, Priscilla behaves as if she whole-heartedly agrees with that premise. She lets remarks about what a good girl I am go by uncorrected, and finds things she can add to the conversation that make it sound like she has been hovering over me all day. It's quite a remarkable performance.

"Take *her* with you," Priscilla tells Daddy. "I haven't got time to look after the baby and clean up after *her* all day. At least Penny tries to help out around here."

It's a Saturday during tax season, and Daddy has to go into his office in

Boston to finish getting the company's tax records prepared because he is the head accountant. Being with him for the day is fine with me. He doesn't raise his voice or get angry. He speaks to me as if he likes me and he listens to what I have to say.

We take the car into the city and ride the elevator way, way far up to his pitch dark office, the only light a weak stream of yellow filtering through the glass door from the hallway. No one else is there. The room is a jumble of desks and chairs. Daddy turns on the long fluorescent lamp on his desk, and sets me up at a nearby table with some paper and colored pens. He finds an old adding machine I can play with, shows me how to use it and talks to me about being careful not to mess up anyone's desk. Then he concentrates very hard on his work.

Despite Priscilla's constant complaints, or maybe because of them, I know a lot about acting like a good girl, according to what the situation demands. I am content to sit quietly, drawing and coloring as Daddy fills his ledgers and gets his adding machine going so fast it's a constant whirrrrd-tap-tap-whirrrrd. Once in a while I get up to show him a drawing or to try out the different swivel chairs that are by the desks scattered around the room.

When it's time for lunch Daddy says, "You stay right here while I go down to the cafeteria in the lobby and grab us a sandwich, OK?" I don't like the idea at all; it's too dark and strange in the office.

"Can I come with you?" I ask.

"You just stay right here. You'll be fine. I'll be right back," he says.

I hear the eerie whine of the elevator leaving, followed by the dead quiet. Then there's the waiting and waiting and waiting, swallowed up by the dark office, stuck like glue to Daddy's still warm chair, all alone and curled up. Finally, there's the whoosh of the elevator coming back.

Daddy comes in with sandwiches and cartons of milk – and many, many straws. "I got you some extra straws just in case," he says. He puts five or six down by my sandwich. I love him for that, for knowing I'm a little kid who might ruin a paper straw just by using it. In case that happens, he makes it okay in advance. No scolding for it, no blame, no put-downs. Just acting like a good father.

I've woken up so early it's still dark outside. The bedroom I share with Penny is pitch black. I roll over to look over at the shadow of my sleeping sister. The ends of my hair feel like brush bristles poking into my cheek. Both Penny and I have short hair now. Priscilla said she doesn't have time to fuss over long hairdos before sending her girls off to school every morning, now that there is a baby to take care of. The new look and feel is hard to get used to, but it's just as well; she could be rough getting the snarls out.

I start thinking about my predicament, turning as usual to the question of how to be good enough to change Priscilla's attitude towards me. Does Penny ever try to imagine what it would be like to wake up some day and discover that our roles have reversed and I have suddenly become the good girl in Priscilla's eyes? If I were in her shoes I'd be scared stiff about things like that. In my shoes, I fantasize about it all the time.

An idea starts to take shape in that dark before dawn. Penny's job is to set the table for breakfast and supper. Penny is a good girl. If I set the table for breakfast, will I be a good girl? She's sound asleep and I'm wide awake, so why not?

Convincing myself that this is a really good idea, I dress stealthily in the dark and sneak downstairs. Turning on the dining room light, I look at the table and try to imagine the collection of things that need to be there for breakfast. I get them all from their places in the kitchen – dishes, napkins, silverware – and put everything on the table by each person's place. Quietly; oh, so quietly. Oops! Forgot the hot pad for the coffee pot! Now it looks right. Wait! The butter dish and the sugar bowl! Finally I sit still in a chair against the dining room wall, looking over my work again and again to see if I've missed anything, waiting for people to get up.

Priscilla comes down in her robe and slippers with Stephen in her arms.

"Well! What have you been up to?" she says, glancing at the table before she heads into the kitchen to put Stephen in his high chair.

"I set the table," I say, keeping my head down, poised for flight in case she gets mad at me for making noise or doing something I'm not supposed to do.

"Well." She seems stuck for words. "Have you finally decided to be a good girl?" she says. Whoa. I think I did it. I finally got her to look at me differently. The thought subdues, rather than elates.

Meekly I say, "Yes."

I stay in the chair and out of her way until everyone is downstairs and ready to eat. Daddy is proud of me and delighted to see that Priscilla is pleased with my behavior for a change. He thinks his prayers have finally brought peace, love and happiness to his family. "You did such a good job!" he says.

"Ya, well. She forgot the salt and pepper," Priscilla says meanly. My face falls. But Daddy won't let her spoil the moment. While I leave to get the salt and pepper from the kitchen counter he says to her,

"That's OK. She was being helpful and doing a good job and that's what's important." Priscilla, of all things, agrees.

"That's right," she says. "Now," turning to me, "let's see if you can keep it up."

I ride the wave of maternal approval all the way through the Kindergarten morning, and then race to get home for lunch on time, even though I suspect that Priscilla must have already lost her good will towards me on one lousy excuse or another. But I am wrong.

After lunch, as I head upstairs for my nap, she follows me from the kitchen to the living room. She usually doesn't have conversations with me, but today she wants to tell me something. "Look," she says, pointing to a little basket of Easter candies on top of the piano. "Grammie and I got these for you today. They're just for you, for being a good girl."

I start to wonder how Grammie got involved, since she's not even here today, then suddenly I absorb the fact of Priscilla's nearness. She is bending down to me. She never bends down to talk to me, so her posture feels exquisitely loving. The ogre/dragon lady/cruel witch might be melding into a mother. The candy means little in comparison. "When you get up from your nap," Priscilla says, "you can have some."

I need a nap today. Usually I'm so wide awake I can only lie quietly for a few minutes. Then I start calling out through the closed door, "Mum, Can I get up? Mum, Can I get up?" over and over until it sounds like "Mumkinlgeddup, Mumkinlgeddup," with no inflection and barely a breath in between, until Priscilla gives in and calls up the stairs,

"You can get up now, Susan." But today I'm blissed out with all this motherly attention. I'm also exhausted from waking up so early. In that muddle of feelings I enhance my good girl reputation for the day by sleeping for a couple of hours.

Afterwards, Priscilla helps me pick out candies from the basket on the piano and we go outside. *We* go outside. This is so bizarre. After all the longing and fantasizing about what it would be like to have my mother treating me like a normal daughter, it's awkward to be interacting with Priscilla as if we have been doing this all along. I should be awash in relief and joy, but the day feels surreal. Part of me is holding myself off to one side, a detached observer, wary about what might come next.

I walk around and around the wooden edge of the sandbox, eating my candy and balancing like I'm on a tightrope wire, stopping with both feet on each of the four triangular seats at the corners. While Priscilla takes the morning laundry off the clothesline, I chatter about all the news I can think of.

"In school today the teacher had a tray with all these different things on it, like a paper clip, an eraser, some scissors, a pencil – stuff like that. Then she put a towel over it and took something out and we had to guess what was missing. I always got it right!"

"Uh-huh," Priscilla says. I think she's trying, too. I mean, I think she's trying, like me, to keep our good girl day going.

Still walking around the sandbox edge, "Hope told me her family is getting a boy!" I tell her excitedly. "They're adopting a Korean boy. I think he's three years old. So she's going to have a brother, too."

"Really?" says Priscilla. "Well they do have a lot of girls."

"That's what Hope said. They have all girls and wanted a boy."

I make it through the rest of the day in Priscilla's good graces, although she rejects the good night kiss as usual, saying, "You need to show me that you can keep this going." When she comes upstairs to tuck us in, it's kisses for Penny and, "Good night, Dear," to Penny and nothing for me, as usual. Before she closes the door, though, she says to me, "Now wasn't that better? Let's hope you can keep it up." Shucks. I had imagined a perfect ending, one with a mother's caress and lots of praise.

In the days to come, I sleep until Daddy wakes us up for school and miss all my chances to set the table. Priscilla acts as if my not setting the table means I've gone back to my evil ways. And anyway, that's Penny's job. I'm sure she doesn't want me upsetting her applecart. I'm left with a gem of a memory for the memento box, and that's it.

School-Aged Blues

I wear my obsessive quest for good girl status like an invisible cloak. It's what I'm doing every waking minute of every day, but no one can tell. On the outside, I look like a serious child, withdrawn and solemn. Inside, I'm making sure that anything that could evoke Priscilla's criticism or cause her to punish me is on my radar miles in advance. I think if I'm careful I can avoid situations that might set her off, although I can't remember a single thing I've seen coming.

I am also a six-year-old first grader who escapes from the gravity of her family circumstances by playing with other children. When I am with other kids I get immersed in the moment, wrapped up in conversations or games of hop scotch we have on the way to and from school each day. This is not something I can afford to do.

Priscilla has given me a specific time to be home for lunch and to be home after school, and if I am not there at those exact moments, she spanks me on the bottom with the hairbrush for every minute I am late. The same thing happens if she tells me I can go over to Hope's house to play for one hour. No matter what I do, I seem to be late enough every day and in every situation that I get the hairbrush on my backside.

To be thruthful, sometimes I do dawdle with Paul and Hope on the way home from school, joking around with them at the top of their street before I walk on to Prince Ave. Priscilla's hairbrush hangs over me like a lead ball on a frayed rope, yet I prolong the enjoyable moments with friends before facing her wrath.

Mostly, though, I do focus on this demand to be home at a certain time and I do everything I can to meet it. But I'm astonished to walk in the back door every day and find Penny already seated at the little table in the kitchen, waiting for her lunch or her afternoon snack. No matter what I do, I get the hairbrush. It takes me a long time to figure out that Penny's third grade class leaves by the door closest to Highland Ave, while the first grade classes are dismissed from a door on the far side of the building. She has a good five-minute head start! That wouldn't matter to Priscilla anyway. A rule is a rule. It's not worth kicking up a fuss.

Penny must have given this some thought, though. One Tuesday, the day of her piano lesson, she says to me on the way back to school after lunch, "Why don't you try to get a ride with me and my piano teacher after school today. She's always there waiting for me, and she could give us both a ride home. But you have to be on time. She won't wait."

I leap at the chance, thinking about it throughout the afternoon and then racing across the schoolyard after school so I can catch the car waiting at the curb. Halfway across the playground I fall headlong onto a stony patch of ground. As I struggle to get back up, the car pulls away. My reward for trying to get home on time is a pair of scraped hands and a huge gash in my leg that is creating a very bloody sock. Now Priscilla is going to be mad about the sock and mad about having to clean up the injury, in addition to being mad about my late arrival. All I can do is cry.

I've become a thief. This behavior comes over me the way the shadow of a cloud cloaks a hillside. One Saturday when the family is shopping in the five-and-ten I pocket a gaudy ring with a big red stone. Then, unable to keep it to myself and wanting to wear the thing, I become a liar as well, making up some fantastic story about how I got it.

Priscilla sends me to my room with no lunch. She sends Daddy up later to give me a spanking. Daddy has never spanked anyone and doesn't much care for that part. He looks silly sitting on the child's chair as he lectures me and works himself up to bending me over his knee and giving me a few wallops. I cry my eyes out. He takes me back to the five-and-ten and makes me give the ring back and apologize to the manager.

Time After Time

At school our classrooms seem to always have a half a dozen Red Cross boxes lined up on a shelf in the back of the room – navy blue cardboard boxes, about the size of a bread pan, with the red and white Red Cross symbol on the sides. We collect things to send to servicemen or war survivors or victims of disasters. One day I spy a wrist watch in one of the boxes. It has a black elastic band and a gold case around the dial. I think it is beautiful. When the class goes outside for recess, I dawdle long enough to pocket the watch.

I can't help flaunting it to my classmates, though. "Look what my parents bought for me!" Of course, the child who brought in the watch for the collection recognizes the lie immediately and tells the teacher. I spend a rough time locked in a stall in the in the girl's room bawling out of terror over what will happen to me. The teacher finally goes and gets Penny out of her class to come and calm me down. But having Penny witness my shame is almost as bad as if they'd sent for Priscilla. My sister has no sympathy for me, just wants me to stop blubbering. I know I'll catch hell when I go home.

Nevertheless, I can't keep my eyes off a shiny red delicious apple that is nestled one day in a collection box. Again I dawdle when the other children go out to recess. Then I eat the apple as fast as I can, taking huge bites and swallowing them before they're completely chewed.

I make it home for lunch, but can't eat anything, the apple sitting uneasily on my guilty stomach. When it comes up in great big chunks it is so obvious, Priscilla says, "Where'd you get the apple?"

"A friend at school gave it to me," I say, the liar colluding once again with the thief.

She is suspicious, but doesn't press further. I go back to school, telling Priscilla that throwing up made me feel fine again.

That episode finally exorcises the liar and the thief; the cloud passes by. No stealing or lying from here on. I devote myself to cute Billy Partridge, a newcomer at school whose father is in the service. His frequent transfers leave Billy lonesome for permanent friends. Every recess Billy wants to play catch with me and only me, so we hog the big red rubber kickball. We just seem to have a bond.

Priscilla and Daddy are out doing their many errands. Grammie is puttering around – cleaning up from breakfast, picking up Stephen's toys, stacking magazines. A brown and white striped wool jersey that Penny got for Christmas is neatly folded and placed with a stack of other Christmas presents, beside the wing-backed chair by the fireplace. As Grammie starts to sweep the hearth, her broom accidentally jostles the little kerosene pitcher there, splashing some of its contents onto Penny's new jersey.

"Don't say anything to your mother now," Grammie admonishes us as she picks up the shirt and examines it. "Phew, that stinks! Pete will never forgive me for ruining a brand new shirt. It's wool, too. Going to be tough to get that out. Just run along you two. Get your things on and go out and play. I'll clean this up and she'll never know." She takes the shirt to the kitchen sink and starts pulling cleaners out of the cupboard.

Penny can't get over this. We're bundled up in snow suits, boots, scarfs and mittens, shivering by the cinder block incinerator Daddy built in the back yard for burning trash and having cookouts. "Isn't that lying?" she asks, all confused. "If we don't tell Mummy what happened, that's just like lying."

"I don't know," I say. "I think lying would be if Grammie tells her that one of us knocked it over. You know which one of us she'd blame, too."

"It's not right," Penny says. Her face is all squinched up like she has a headache. "I don't think that's right, to pretend it didn't happen. I want to tell Mummy."

When we go back inside, Grammie is still standing at the kitchen sink, working on the shirt. "It's too cold out there," I tell her. "We had to come in."

"Then go play down cellar," Grammie says. "I want you two out of the way while I'm working on this."

Penny is so tense about the situation she can't get into playing. "Go upstairs and talk to Grammie, then," I finally tell her. "Ask her if she thinks it's like lying."

Penny goes upstairs and asks Grammie her burning question, only to be told, "It's none of your business, young lady. Now get back down stairs."

After Daddy and Priscilla come back with the groceries and we're all sitting around the dining table having lunch, Grammie tells the story of spilling kerosene on Penny's new shirt and how she's been working to clean it. She brings it to the table to show Priscilla, saying, "I think I got the smell out. Can you smell anything, Pete?"

Priscilla takes a whiff. "Whew," she says. "Just give the shirt to Susan."

I live in a constant state of anxiety about what I'll have to cope with next. The toughest circumstances happen when I innocently expect something because it seems like the kind of thing kids take for granted, especially if my sister Penny has it. Whether it's a Halloween costume, membership in the Mickey Mouse Club, or a ride on the Ferris wheel at the street fair, if my sister can have it I assume I can have that, too. She's my yardstick for knowing what comes with being a child in this family.

But I'm an idiot for thinking that, when time after time I have to face being treated differently on grounds that Priscilla thinks I am a bad girl.

"First you need to show us you can take care of your things," is what I get from Priscilla.

"You haven't shown us you can be responsible."

"When you learn to do as you're told we'll see about it."

"Why should we let you do that? What have you done to deserve It?"

Consequently, what I see Penny experience has no bearing on my life.

If I can't take my mother's affection for granted I sure as hell can't take for granted that I will have a parent at my school plays, or an afternoon snack waiting for me when I get home from school, or a balloon from the Fourth of July parade, or a turn at popping popcorn in the fireplace, or a popsicle from the Ding Dong truck. I've been so sluggish about realizing this you'd think I was dense as a post. Every object and event around me signifies one more thing that Priscilla can deny me or take away.

The morning I wake up expecting to find my first tooth fairy money under my pillow is a good example. I feel only empty space between the sheet and the pillow case. The tooth is gone but no money is in its place. I am positive that since the tooth has disappeared the money must be around somewhere. So I go looking for it. In a small dish on the table by the front door I spy a bunch of loose change. Ah-ha! I grab it in my fist and run upstairs to my parent's room. "I found this in the dish downstairs!" I say, bouncing up on Daddy's side of the bed. "Do you think this is what the tooth fairy left me?"

"No," says Daddy. "That's for the paper boy. You need to put that back downstairs."

"What makes you think the tooth fairy would leave *you* anything," Priscilla mutters from her side of the bed.

I assume I will wear my Brownie uniform to school when I have Brownie meetings because everyone else in Brownies does, and Penny wears her Girl Scout uniform to school on days when she has Girl Scout meetings. But one day that is taken away. Priscilla says, "I'm not about to spend my time ironing a special dress for you when you do nothing around here to help me."

Every time it's Penny's turn to bring refreshments for her troop, she leaves the house with a tray of luscious looking homemade chocolate cupcakes with whirled crowns of fluffy frosting. When it's my turn to bring refreshments, Priscilla resentfully hands me a cheap package of store bought cookies. Vanilla. The girls ask me why that's all I have.

Priscilla stops signing my birthday cards and holiday cards, "Love, Mum and Dad," the way she signs cards for Penny and Stephen. For me it's just, "Mum and Dad." Over time even that will deteriorate into "M and Dad." I don't think Daddy knows about this because she signs the cards for both of them.

When it's time for the class Valentine's Day party, I know there won't be any cards from me in the big box with the slot on top that the whole class decorated with red hearts and white paper lace. Priscilla will find some oversight on my part that makes her unhappy – a sock under the bed, dirt on my sleeve, a broken barrette – and that will be the end of any hope for cards to give out to my classmates.

If one of the neighborhood moms is taking a car load of kids to the movies, the library or a skating park, I can predict they'll have to count me out. Priscilla doesn't think I deserve to be just one of the kids.

For all of it, I have to make up excuses that reveal nothing of my true situation. You just don't talk about family business to outsiders. Besides, who'd believe me? What would I say? "She won't iron my Brownie uniform." "She won't let me kiss her good night." "She says I'm 'helpless, hopeless, useless' all the time." "She won't let me have any money or pop the popcorn." There is no one thing to say that gives people the whole picture or the true picture. I am tongue-tied at the idea of trying to explain it clearly and simply to anyone. It's so complicated it would take a week to relate everything that has piled up over the years.

My sister and I no longer invite kids inside our house to play, though; my situation with Priscilla is just too weird.

In Sunday School, I am being taught to think of my circumstances, all circumstances, as perfect. If I would just rethink my situation, using Christian Science dogma to perceive my lot as loving and good, I would finally be able to see that it is loving and good. Try as I might, though, the reality is painful.

I get downhearted sometimes, visibly upset by Priscilla's overt hostility. But this family has no tolerance for whiners and complainers. "What's with the sad sack look?" Priscilla asks at times when I think it should be obvious that her relentless meanness has gotten to me. "Wipe that hang dog expression off your face," she says. So now it's becoming ingrained that my expression should reveal nothing of the turmoil I feel.

My grades have been going downhill since Kindergarten. I dread report cards and teacher-parent nights because I get blamed for all of it. It's my fault that I'm not applying myself. It's my fault that I daydream and get behind in my work. If I would pay attention to my teachers the way I am supposed to there is no reason why my grades wouldn't be all A's and B's like Penny's. The teachers tell my parents, "Penny was such a pleasure to work with. I was expecting more from Susan."

I start having the same dream over and over. We are back at the dingy base housing at Fort Devens. I feel an odd sensation in my mouth, run to the kitchen sink, bend over, open my mouth and watch all of my teeth dropping into the sink.

The family of four that moved into this house has become a family of six. Since Grandpa John's death, Grammie sold her house and has been living in a hotel in Boston, storing much of her furniture in our basement. She stays with us so often, though, that the spare bedroom that was going to be for Stephen is used instead as a guest room for her. Stephen sleeps in our parent's room.

Priscilla and Daddy find a new house across town on a shaded side street that has an elementary school on the corner. Everything about the house on Marshall Road is bigger than what we've had. It has a full two floors with a full basement underneath that includes a laundry room, a tool room and a cold storage room. There's a full attic on top that has one large open area and a smaller room off of that. On the ground floor, a screen porch off the living room stretches from front to back, with the garage underneath. Off of the dining room a sunroom juts out with windows on three sides and a view of the big back yard. Even the hallways and entryways are spacious.

I'm bigger, too, at eight years old. I'm not a little girl anymore. Physically, I am tall for my age and thin as a stick. Intellectually, I am bright but often muddle-headed with tension about Priscilla. When she is safely occupied, I can put together a Lincoln Log structure in a flash, whip through puzzles that call for advanced logical thinking and construct mature assessments of the characters and situations that populate the books I read. The downside is that so much of my intelligence is being spent on trying to solve Priscilla that school gets, at best, odd scraps of half-hearted attention.

I don't know what it means to relax. I've become wary and watchful, sensitive to the slightest sound, trying to interpret every foot fall, facial expression and vocal nuance. I'm dealing with my role in the family all the time, in one way or another, without looking upset. I'm tuned into my periphery all day long, constantly keeping track of Priscilla, the family, even the teachers and kids at school. I am no longer a participant in any of it. I can't afford to be. I've got to stay focused on the threat of Priscilla.

Emotionally, I am a whimpering baby, crying for her mother or for someone, anyone, to please act as a mother, care for me and give me some love.

Nevertheless, some fool part of me hopes for the best, time after time. The move to Marshall Road – that could change things, couldn't it? It signals a new beginning for the family. We can start fresh over there and try to do better at this business of family relationships. Priscilla could use the move to learn from past experience, wipe the slate clean and get right with me. I know I could do that with her. I would forgive all that's passed between us in a heartbeat for the chance to begin again as mother and daughter.

Marshall Road

11 Marshall Road, 1954

Grammie, 1954

Priscilla, 1955

Stephen, Susan, Penny; Hampton Beach, NH, 1956

Priscilla, Ed; 1956

Lorraine, 1961

On the Margins

I am going to have a room of my own! At bedtime on the first night in the house on Marshall Road I am told to go to the room at the top of the stairs, and there I see my bed all by itself. A wandering branch of apple tree in full bloom tickles the screen of the open side window – so close I can see the miniature black pompoms and yellow beads of pollen inside each blossom. Their fragrance makes me tipsy with delight. Out my back window, an indigo sky brushed with the golden palette of sunset peeks through the full bloom of two more apple trees in the back yard. Tall, leafy hedges along the back property line cast that sharp emerald green glow that only a clear summer night produces. I feel like I stepped onto an enchanted island.

Sitting cross-legged on my familiar army surplus bunk bed, I'm full of the jitters and exhilarated by the novelty of having a room of my own. The space around my bed looks huge without Penny's matching bunk bed just an arm's length away. My dolls and bags of sewing scraps for making doll clothes are within sight, along with my Doris Day and Rock Hudson paper doll cutout kits. An open box holds my most beloved books – the one about the bunny who finds an Easter egg with a chick inside, a book of Mother West Wind stories, the Grimm's Fairy Tales. Over by the window the pointy tops of my spool looms poke out of another box. I use those for knitting yarn tails that can be coiled into hot pads or braided into miniature rugs. The prayer plaque that has always hung on the wall behind my bed has already been hung in the same spot in this room. "Father-Mother God. Loving me. Guide me while I sleep. Guide my little feet up to Thee."

This room, this place of my own, magically took shape while Penny and Stephen and I stayed outside playing Red Rover and Red Light with a new bunch of neighborhood kids; while we sat on the screen porch eating peanut butter sandwiches on paper plates, taking in the bigness of the space, the steep driveway, the woods across the street and all the other new details.

At one point I spied a watch with a gray wristband on Priscilla's wrist, just like the watch my Aunt Lorraine gave me last Christmas. She hoped it would help me to get home from school on time and avoid the hairbrush. But the watch had been immediately taken away. "Give that to me," Priscilla had said. "Until you can show me that you're going to behave and do what you're told to do, that watch is too good for the likes of you." Now she's wearing it? She couldn't do that to me, could she? Just take my watch and wear it as if it had been given to her? She's a thief! She stole my watch! I managed to work up enough righteous indignation to confront her.

"Is that my watch you're wearing?" I said to her in passing.

"Yes. I needed it to tell the movers when to take their breaks," she said. "Mine is broken." She said all three sentences as if she was talking to a normal person who had every right to ask the question. That made it so easy to keep on believing that things would get better now.

The dusky remaining light of this moving day patiently waits for my eyes to adjust and rove towards the closet in my room. The door is partly open. There on the shelf several games have been stacked, games that belong to the family. I can make out Parcheesi, Chinese Checkers, Mr. Potato Head. What in the world does that mean? These games have always been kept on the built-in shelves of the living room in the house on Prince Ave. I'm not allowed to take them out and play with them; I have to wait to be invited to play when the cousins are over or when Penny wants to play and no one else is around. Were the movers told to put them here to get them out of the way? Are they really mine now? I tiptoe over, stretch up, ever-so-carefully take down Parcheesi and bring it into bed with me.

At the breakfast table I get up the courage to ask Dad, "Am I allowed to play with the games on my closet shelf?"

"Yes," he says. "We decided to split them up between you and Penny because there are no shelves in this living room for them. You need to take good care of them, OK?"

I will also have to devise ways to play each game alone. Priscilla is about to escalate her efforts to make me disappear. But for now, I am enraptured by the novelty of a room of my own and blind to anything it could mean that isn't wonderful.

Sunsets, sweet apple blossoms, and infinite possibilities for enjoying a few moments of quietude are mine; a refuge away from Priscilla's swatting hands and demeaning words, away from Penny's status as the one who can do no wrong, always in contrast to my role as the one who can never do right. It is such a comfort. Every night I creep to the back window, prop a book on the windowsill, and read until I can see no more. I love that room the way we love all gifts magical and unexpected.

Someone is not too pleased with the arrangement of bedrooms. I am told to swap rooms with Penny; no explanation. Penny passes me wordlessly as we carry armloads of books and games and clothes down the long hallway, back and forth.

Rats. She got the Monopoly set.

This room at the front of the house looks out onto the street and the steep, woodsy hill on the other side. Instead of being over the kitchen, I am now over the dining room. The same apple tree is out the side window, the branches brushing the roof of the sunroom. Now when I come upstairs I have to follow the banister down the hallway to the right and then turn right again past the door to the attic. Not bad. I seem to be farther away from whatever action and conversations might be going on downstairs, but that means furtive noises can go undetected as I sneak out of bed to read each night. There's a street lamp on this side! I can read by the light of that for hours! These exquisite moments of solitude still feel like hugs from a fairy godmother. There is no warning that they are about to be fused into unrelenting isolation from everyone else in the family.

Priscilla starts saying, "Susan. Go to your room," after each meal. When I come in from playing she says, "Go to your room." Sometimes she tacks on, "I can't stand the sight of you," or "Haven't you got anything better to do than to stand around and get in the way? Helpless, hopeless, useless." She sees me reading one afternoon on the screen porch, the place I most love to be. Hands on hips, she says, "What do you think you're doing out here? Go to your room." I come in from the yard to get a drink of water at the kitchen sink. I am greeted with, "What do you think you're doing? Go to your room."

She says these lines so often that within a matter of weeks I don't need the cue. If I am in the house I am supposed to stay in my room unless otherwise directed. Priscilla calls me downstairs when it is time to eat breakfast. Priscilla calls me downstairs when it is time to eat supper. I'm not supposed to be meandering around downstairs before mealtimes. I'm not allowed to stay downstairs after supper, to go into the living room with everyone else to chat and watch TV. "What have you done to deserve TV?" Priscilla says. "Go to your room."

Only three weeks remain in the school year after our move to Marshall Road. Reading and math groups are winding down. Blocks of the school day are increasingly filled by going out to the playground with sketchpads and chalk, or watercolors so muddied by multiple users every color in the box looks brown. If my new third grade class isn't outside depicting the spring scenery, we are inside doing end-of-the-year classroom clean-up activities.

One day the teacher sends me to an office down the hall, where a tired old man with big, jiggly jowls dwarfs the little room, the child's chair, and the table where I am instructed to sit. He spreads out his collection of pattern blocks, word lists and sequence cards with pictures. A stopwatch is curled inside the palm of his hand, his fat thumb working the start and stop buttons.

The questions he asks are easy as pie, until he takes a set of wooden jigsaw-like puzzle pieces out of a box and instructs me to "put these together to form an organ of the body." How I struggle with those pieces! I want to make them into an organ just like the organ at my new friend Ruthie's house – with top and bottom rows of black and white keys, pearly buttons to pull out and wooden foot pedals. Try as I might, I can't do it. When he clicks the stopper on his stupid stopwatch and rapidly puts the pieces together in front of me on the table to show me that the picture is of a hand, I am both ashamed and indignant. How utterly unfair! A hand is not an organ!

A few days later when Dad comes home from work, Priscilla tells him that the school called her and said my IQ is extremely high. They want my parents to think about placing me in the accelerated fourth grade class the next year. Eavesdropping on this conversation from my bedroom, I am stunned. Priscilla is talking about me, or at least my brain, with what sounds like genuine interest. She seems either impressed by or proud of my IQ; I can't decide which. However, since grades are the ultimate litmus test of intelligence as far as Priscilla and Ed are concerned, and my grades are consistently mediocre, I am slated for fall placement in the regular fourth grade class.

I go out every morning as soon as the dew evaporates enough to keep my sneakers dry. There are many children in this neighborhood, and it is summer. If my new friends haven't wandered over to our yard, I ask permission to go to Ruthie's house down the street or to Gail's on the corner, knowing the neighborhood gang often starts out at one place or the other. I ask Priscilla if I can go across the street to the school playground so I can look for friends there. When kids are away on their summer vacations, I take a book outside and climb up the apple tree next to the house; it's a perfect tree for sitting in the crook of a branch, reading. The bark is cool, dark and smooth, the branches easy to climb. Priscilla would much rather have me out of the house anyway, as long as I don't think I am allowed to be just like any other kid.

I am not allowed to ride Penny's bicycle, or the bicycles of any of my friends. Penny has a new, black, three-speed English bike; her old green bike sits beside it in the cellar, unused. I'm way too big for the tricycle now, but Priscilla rejects the idea of letting me use Penny's old bike or giving me one of my own. "You don't deserve a bike," she says. "Don't let me catch you riding Ruthie's over in the schoolyard, either."

Some days I'm not allowed to play in the shade. "You stay in the sun, you hear me? If I catch you in the shade you'll get the hairbrush." That one is really tough to explain to my friends.

Priscilla decides that when I go to the schoolyard, I have to always be where she can see me if she stands out on our front walk, which means Ruthie and I can no longer design floor plans for doll houses by scooping together pine needles in the cool, dark woods adjacent to the playground. I have to "come when called" – the first time. If my friends and I are in the middle of a boisterous game of jump rope on the hardtop at the far end of the playground and I miss hearing that first call, I am whacked with the hairbrush and lose permission to play with anyone. I swear sometimes Priscilla deliberately doesn't raise her voice enough for me to hear it.

Any misstep justifies punishments I am already being given. The order of the universe seems to be effect precedes cause, not the other way around. I'm not allowed free access to the house because yesterday I didn't come when called the first time, proving that I don't mind my mother. I have to be punished by staying in my room when I am inside the house, even though I have been told to stay in my room since the day we moved here. I'm not to assume I have the right to go out on the porch the way Penny and Stephen do, or play in the living room the way Penny and Stephen do, because I need to learn to mind my mother and she's told me to stay in my room.

Priscilla brings dessert to the table, looks at me and says spitefully, "You don't deserve dessert. Go get an apple from the refrigerator." After a few days, this, too, is a ritual. "Did you have your apple today? No? I didn't think so. Go get an apple. You don't deserve dessert." Dad, Penny and Stephen look on silently. Does this make sense to them? No one else has to have an apple every day.

New rules like this always set in motion the process of examining my options and making decisions about whether or not I can do anything to avoid having the rule imposed. Should I ask for an apple during the day to avoid the dessert scenario? No. Priscilla would talk about my not appreciating the way my father's hard-earned money goes to feeding me every day. She would tell me there's no reason for me to be helping myself to the refrigerator and eating her out of house and home in between meals. Should I ask her to give me an apple with my lunch? No. She'd tell me I'd better be grateful for whatever I get, since I don't do anything to earn my keep around here and she has enough to do without catering to my demands.

No one can say she doesn't do things especially for me, though. When the rhubarb in her garden is in season, Priscilla serves rhubarb pie with ice cream for dessert, and makes a separate batch of plain rhubarb sauce. I'm not allowed to have the pie, but I can have the sauce instead of an apple. Rhubarb sauce makes my mouth pucker so bad that Dad gets a kick out of watching me eat it, laughing and saying, "Tart enough for you there?" It wouldn't occur to him that this rule, like all the others, is bent, warped, crazy-making. He wouldn't dream of asking Priscilla why I'm not allowed to have the pie and must have the sauce instead. He's thinking what a good mother she is to make me a special batch of sauce.

I come to believe that I'm lucky Priscilla is still allowing me to join the family for meals, so I eat what is put in front of me and don't dare ask for second helpings, or butter for my bread, or more milk from the pitcher, or even salt and pepper. I don't want to ask someone to pass me something only to be told I don't deserve it.

I go downstairs to say a perfunctory good night before going to bed. Priscilla is sitting on the couch, knitting. She growls at me without even raising her head, "You're to brush your teeth from now on with the bicarbonate of soda that's in the medicine cabinet up there. You don't deserve to use the toothpaste." Dad sits in his recliner in silence, reading his Christian Science Quarterly.

Preoccupations

My parents are busy papering and painting the dining room. They replace our worn maple dining set with a very elegant cherry table and matching chairs with damask covers. A huge new cherry sideboard and hutch takes up one whole wall of the dining room. Between that and the built-in china cabinet on another wall, many silver and china serving pieces are now out of storage and on display behind glass cabinet doors.

The old maple dining set goes to the screen porch, where a glider that once belonged to Grammie has been placed, along with a fancy new charcoal grille that Dad uses on summer Saturdays.

Penny gets a new girlie bed and we each get new bureaus.

The sunroom off of the dining room gets a face lift as well, with a fresh coat of paint and new carpeting, although no one seems to go in there very much. I would like to. The windows all around make it light and airy. I can see it has very comfortable-looking easy chairs, including a wingback and one of those lounging chairs that tilts back. What I can't see without going inside is that a bed has been placed along the wall on the dining room side.

A carpenter comes to build a wall upstairs to divide the master bedroom that runs from front to back over the living room. Stephen, still a little guy of 4, has been sharing that room with my parents, his cot set up at one end and the Lionel train set my father assembled for him taking up a ton of floor space in the middle. My parent's room is now going to be on the back end of that space, with a full-length closet along the dividing wall. The train set is going down cellar on a plywood table Dad made for it. Stephen's room is going to be on the front end, right across the hall from mine.

Dad and Priscilla paper Stephen's room with red Scottish plaid paper on three walls. The fourth wall is papered with a repeating pattern of male sports figures: a golfer, a football player and a baseball player. They are all in action, doing their sport, and I suppose the message is that Stephen, as the only boy, should be active and physical like those role models, even though our father has not been like that since he was a Boy Scout in his teens. Those images are so not like Stephen, who prefers watching Ding Dong School and Romper Room, or sitting on people's laps.

Stephen and I devise quiet games of flicking wadded up balls of paper at each other as we sit in our respective doorways. We look at the pages of his picture books across the divide of the hallway. We make goofy faces until one of us has to crack up. Priscilla soon realizes that she does not like this arrangement. If she hears Stephen and me whispering to each other she comes into the hallway downstairs and yells up through the open space, "You stay away from her, Stephen! One of her is bad enough!"

I don't think Stephen thinks much about Priscilla one way or the other. He's so easy-going he seems to take her personality into account and then go on his merry way. "He lives in his own world," people say. "He's just a happy-go-lucky boy." He's definitely a winner in the inclusion-exclusion game of chance, though. Priscilla likes him and mothers him. He's a bona fide member of her ideal immediate family: herself, Dad, Penny and Stephen.

Priscilla stops me on my after-school walk of practiced invisibility as I make my way through the kitchen and on up to my room. She says, "Your Grandmother's in the living room. You go say hello."

Grammie is sitting on the couch, surrounded by boxes. She unpacks a box as she chats with Penny and Stephen. "I'm going to put this in my room," she says, referring to a small crystal bowl she's inspecting before setting it down gently on the end table. She reaches back into the box at her feet and pulls out a bronze statuette, about a foot high. It depicts a little girl in a bonnet, standing on a chair, holding one untied shoe. "Put this on the mantelpiece for me, Penny. This was always on the mantelpiece in my house." Penny puts it up on the mantle, next to the clock with the face like a ship's helm that chimes the quarter hours in ship's bells. Then Grammie carefully unfolds a yellowed piece of coarse, fragile paper. On it is a drawing of that statuette. "Your mother did this at the age of 5," Grammie says. Guided only by one-inch grid lines on the graph paper, the drawing is unbelievably precise for a 5-year-old. "Pete was very talented. She could draw anything. I could never bear to throw this out."

The drawing is stunning. I love hearing about a childhood experience of Priscilla's. It's nice to be included in the moment. However, I am beginning to feel the slow suffusion of shock. It's a relief when Priscilla comes to the doorway to say, "Susan. Go to your room."

Grammie is going to live with us? She is a moody, nasty person. To this day, Priscilla, her oldest child, is the only person who can do no wrong in her eyes, and Auntie Belle, the middle child in her family, can do no right. Grammie constantly puts down her youngest child and only son, my Uncle Bud, because he is poor, married a Catholic, and prefers to work with his hands instead of sitting at a desk doing a white collar job like my father. Just about everyone Grammie encounters is subject to her extremely harsh judgments and prejudices.

Quite often Grammie compares me to Auntie Belle. My hair is light like Auntie Belle's. Sometimes the phrases I meant to say as a little kid came out backward ("look at the chimney coming out of smoke!"), like Auntie Belle used to do when she was little. I choose the wrong friends, just like Auntie Belle did. I'm skinny, clumsy, careless, lazy, disobedient, messy and on and on and on, "just like Isabel." Having Grammie around on a permanent basis does not bode well for me.

The roof of the sunroom beckons to me in my desperation. Can I make it out my window, creep down onto a branch of the apple tree, and run far, far away? I have about thirty cents. Nine more years before I can leave home; nine more years of coping with Priscilla. And now Grammie, too? It is too much to contemplate.

Not long after Grammie's arrival, Priscilla just has to play musical bedrooms one more time. Stephen moves to the top of the stairs where I had first been and then Penny. Penny moves back to her original room, which has just been my room. I am told to move to the room across the hall from Penny, into Stephen's room, the one with the plaid and the male sports figures on the wall. For the next nine years, wallpaper and all, that is my childhood bedroom.

Early in the year, we are given a note to take home to inform our parents that this school has a band and an orchestra for students in fourth through sixth grades. Music teachers come to school once a week to give lessons on the various instruments. It's an enrichment opportunity for those who are interested.

I'm so excited I speak up at the dinner table. "I really want to take piano lessons," I tell the stone face sitting across from me, imagining that since we have a piano and Penny had lessons for a couple of years when she was my age, my wishes have a chance of being in sync with the possibility. What am I thinking? Priscilla will invite me into the living room after supper each night, where I will gather everyone around the piano to sing popular songs and show tunes? She can't even bear to put my school picture on the damn piano! Photos of Penny and Stephen are the only ones up there.

When the permission slip shows up by my breakfast plate the next morning, I smile all the way to school. Before I turn it in, I take a quick peek to make sure it has a signature, and it does.

Those of us taking orchestra lessons get called down to the music room for the first time a few days later. I sit happily chatting with the girl next to me while the conductor hands out instruments. I know that pretty soon he'll call me over to the piano that sits on the far side of the room. But when he comes around to me, he puts a battered black rounded case on my lap with some oddly shaped thing inside. "What's this?" I ask.

"It's a viola," he says.

Time After Time

"What's a viola?"

"It's what you're parents checked off on the permission slip," he says.

OK. Big mental leap required. If I want to be in the orchestra and play an instrument, I guess I'm playing viola.

A couple of months later, the conductor calls Priscilla to tell her I am ahead of the other students and need private lessons. Mr. Janis comes to our house once a week for the next three years. He and I meet right after school, standing by the upright piano in the living room so that he can keep us in tune and play duets with me. He's a concert violinist, always brings his violin to show me ways of making notes sound pure and sweet. Sometimes he'll even play a whole piece for me, either on his violin or on my viola, which is like having a private concert.

If he wonders why I am notable by my absence in the photo display right there, he never says a word. Priscilla hands him a check on his way out without grousing about the expense or threatening to take this activity away as one more thing I don't deserve.

My parents buy me a decent viola to use instead of the beaten-up school instrument. I cherish the tawny brown wood with the S-shaped sound holes and the scrolled neck, the mocha brown case, the chocolate brown velvet lining, the green satin pocket for rosin with a ribbon tab for lifting the cover, the holder for the padded chin rest, the holder for the bow. I love the all of it. Once in a while, when I am practicing up in my room after lunch or after school, Grammie comes to the open stairway and calls up in a soft and mellow voice, "Play that one again, Susan. I like that one."

Although I can sing, our household is not a world where one can burst into song for any reason, let alone use vocal music to express pent up feelings. The voice is too dangerous a tool. Instrumental music, however, is a safe, accepted route to the affective dimensions of life. Grandpa Daniel was a concert pianist. Grammie made sure all three of her children took instrumental lessons when they were children. Dad and Priscilla belong to the Longines Symphonette Society, which sends new classical records to our house every month. Dad often puts a stack of those records on the new console stereo system on Sunday afternoons, so I have been hearing classical music even when I am confined to my room.

Now it is mine: mine to create and mine to master. The lively and the loving, the angry and the morose, the beautiful and the abhorrent, and so many, many more shades and nuances of feelings I've experienced are all there for safekeeping in the classical repertoire. It doesn't matter which piece Mr. Janis gives me to practice, the viola brings me out of the clay of constipated feelings and into a world where my inexpressible emotions can be heard.

My parents preach the same sermon with every quarterly report card. "As long as you three kids get good grades in Conduct and Effort, we know you're trying. That's the most important thing." Stephen isn't even in school yet, but he sits wide-eyed at the dining table trying to make sense of this lecture that Penny and I get over and over again. "You need to pay attention to your teachers. Behave. Do what they ask you to do. You're not going to get anywhere without trying."

The problem is that each teacher has her own definition of what is meant by the terms "conduct" and "effort." They are catch-all phrases for the things students do that annoy teachers, a place where they can vent their frustrations at having aspects of the learner that are beyond the reach of the grading system. I open that brown report card envelope every time as if I am going to be happily surprised, but every time I am marked down on both Conduct and Effort, and not because I act up. I simply can't apply myself to the work at hand. "She isn't working up to her potential," teachers write. "Susan daydreams instead of getting her work done. She makes careless errors."

Part of the problem is vision. I failed the eye exam given to every student at the end of the third grade, and I do worse and worse on it every year after that as my world turns more and more blurry. But when the note goes home from school each year, Priscilla refuses to send me to an eye doctor for glasses. Penny already wears them, so it isn't Dad's Christian Science beliefs that are standing in the way. It's me, my evil being and undeserving nature.

"Your father and I aren't spending good money on the likes of you. What have you ever done around here to help out?" Priscilla says. She gnaws on her animosity like a piece of gristle that's stuck in her teeth. "You haven't got the sense you were born with. How many times do we have to tell you to get your grades up? We've told you over and over that you need to show improvement in your grades. We shouldn't have to tell you again. There's no sense in us paying good money for glasses if you're not going to apply yourself to your school work." I'll be in the eighth grade before she relents, and she relents only because she finally gets it that my vacuuming and dusting suffer more from not being able to see than from carelessness.

With or without vision issues, I don't live up to teachers' expectations because I can't give more than a scant portion of my brain to school. Textbooks, history, science, times tables, cursive writing – what does any of that matter in relation to my life at home? Mind, soul, and body have been commandeered by an endless preoccupation with studying Priscilla, trying to solve Priscilla, and surviving Priscilla for another day.

I especially hate days when my school class goes on a field trip. All children have to have a signed permission slip to go on excursions to the Museum of Science, Paul Revere's house, Bunker Hill, the state capitol building, the House of the Seven Gables, and many other historic and cultural sites that are close by. But on those mornings, as the other children chatter excitedly about the upcoming trip and the pocket money they have to spend and the lunch and snacks they're bringing, I sit with my hands folded at my desk and my jacket on, waiting to be dismissed, for I do not have permission to go.

When the class files out and onto the big yellow school bus, I walk home across a deserted playground and go up to my room. "Susan," Priscilla says tonelessly from the bottom of the stairs at lunch time. I go down to the dining room to eat my sandwich alone at the dining table. Priscilla, Grammie and Stephen have their lunch in the living room while watching a game show on TV. When the approximate time the class is due back comes around, Priscilla intones my name again. "Susan. Get your coat on and get back there to your classroom. NOW." I walk over to school for the last few minutes of the day, trying to be invisible at my desk in the back of the room as various children waggle their hands in the air and nearly pop out of their seats in their eagerness to answer the teacher's questions about their favorite parts of the field trip.

My fourth grade teacher, Mrs. Milliken, acts from time to time as if she perceives that something at home might be amiss. She is lenient with me when I fall behind in my work. She makes sure that I sit close to the blackboard. If a kind word has been spoken to me in a day, it has come from her.

On a wintery morning I leave for school completely unaware that I am sick. First of all, I am supposed to be a Christian Scientist. I've had practice not letting signs of illness intrude into my consciousness. Secondly, Grammie has been in the hospital, returning to us with bruises the size of grapefruits all over her hands and arms from where the needles have been. She hasn't joined us for dinner the past few days. Her care consumes Priscilla; any fool can see that she does not have an ounce of time or strength or patience to deal with a sick child.

I go to school out of habit, realizing only as I am climbing the stairs to my classroom with all the other children that I am going to be violently ill. I race into the girl's bathroom, just in time to spew a mess into one of the stalls. I wipe off my face and my clothes as best I can with paper towels from the dispenser, then walk away from it and into my classroom across the hall as if nothing has happened. I go to the coat closet, take off my boots, hang up my leggings and jacket, and sit down at my desk.

There are certain things the whole class does together in the mornings: taking attendance, collecting milk money, saying the pledge of allegiance, singing a patriotic song. I spend all of that time sneezing uncontrollably. One after another after another. It's embarrassing. The principal comes in. "Someone has been sick in the girl's room. Do you know anyone who was sick?" We all shake our heads no. I keep sneezing. A boy sitting near me has a box of tissues on his desk. Mrs. Milliken asks him if he could pass it down to me and just let me keep it for a while.

Reading groups come next. I try and try to do my assignments as Mrs. Milliken works with a small group in the corner. Finally I put my head down on my outstretched arm, just for a minute. It feels so heavy. Mrs. Milliken calls me over. "Don't you think you've tried hard enough and you could go home now?" she says, putting her arm around me. I can't resist the kindness in her voice so I just nod, giving in. I go back to my desk, put my things away, get dressed, and head home across the playground. Apparently the principal has already called Priscilla to tell her I am coming, and letting her know that they think I was sick at school.

"The school says someone was sick but won't admit it. Was that you?" she greets me with.

"No. I just don't feel well."

"Then I don't understand why you need to be home. I have enough to do around here without having to take care of you if you're not sick. I guess you'd better spend the rest of the day in bed, hadn't you."

I realize I don't feel that sick anymore, and feel ashamed.

Aunt Lorraine

"Time up!" Dad says as he opens my bedroom door, in his pajamas, fresh out of bed. "Time up!" he says as he opens Penny's door across the hall. "Time up!" he says as he opens Stephen's door down the other end of the hall, then he goes to the bathroom for his morning shower and shave. I hear Priscilla get up, slide her closet door open, put on her bathrobe and slippers and head for the stairs.

Although I can see daylight behind the drawn shades, it looks gray outside. Blech. I am all stuffed up, my head like a ball of soggy towels stuffed into a sack, dripping and dripping. Given Dad's Christian Science and Priscilla's preoccupation with Grammie's frequent ailments, a cold is just one more thing to suffer in silence. I get out from under the covers and go to the front window to raise the shade so I can get an idea of what to wear on this dreary spring day.

"Oh boy! Aunt Lorraine is here!" The sight of her two-toned blue Ford sedan parked at the curb right in front of the house makes my heart leap with joy. The world suddenly sparkles and pops. Gone is the anxiety and dread I wake to every day, replaced by an infusion of utter happiness. Aunt Lorraine is like a movie star to me. Her personality makes everyone happy. She even has an effect on the way Priscilla treats me – a lot of the overt meanness stops – which says a lot about Aunt Lorraine. She could charm an ogre into being nice.

I'm smiling, damning the stuffy head, willing it to go away while I search my closet for something special to wear. When Aunt Lorraine is here, I feel special. Once she gave me a copy of her business photo, a black and white studio portrait that I keep in my wallet. She wrote on the back in her elegant cursive writing, "Love to my favorite and best girl, Lorraine." I am special in her eyes. She lets me know that.

I know it's just a fantasy, but I tell myself Aunt Lorraine could be my real mother. When I was 4 years old I already loved her so much her presence in the house penetrated my sleep one night. I woke up and heard her melodious laughter downstairs. That was all I needed. I got up, convinced myself that it was morning in spite of the darkness, got myself completely dressed – jeans, pink sweater with the pom-pom ties, socks and sneakers – and headed for the stairs. Three adult heads looked up at me from the bottom. Daddy's and Aunt Lorraine's faces were grinning from ear to ear. Not Priscilla's. "What are you doing up?" asked Priscilla in that mean voice stripped of welcome.

"I'm coming down for breakfast," I said, looking happily at Aunt Lorraine's beautiful face.

"Hi, Sweetie!" she said.

"It's the middle of the night," said Priscilla crossly. "You get yourself back into bed young lady."

"Oh, we can just have a quick hello hug, right?" said Aunt Lorraine. "Come on down here Sweetie and let me give you a hug, then you can get right back into bed. We'll see each other in the morning." Down the stairs I went to melt into Aunt Lorraine's arms for one of her super-loving hugs. Oh, if only Daddy and Aunt Lorraine were my parents!

That night I dreamt that I could float on air, my feet inches above the ground. I floated down the stairs and into the dining room. I put my arms out like an airplane and banked right or left at will. I floated outside and up the steep street and around the yard. It felt heavenly.

She's here! Fantastic. Of course, I know the rules. I will have to wait until Priscilla calls me down for breakfast. I can't just go flinging myself at Aunt Lorraine, telling her how overjoyed I am to see her. It's so unfair to have to stay upstairs and listen to everyone else talking with her. I blow my stuffy nose a hundred times. Finally, the signal, "Susan," is barely uttered by Priscilla at the bottom of the stairs.

Time After Time

Aunt Lorraine is ready for me, standing at the dining table, arms open wide, enfolding me against her buxom warmth. How lovely to have my presence greeted with a hug. She's wearing a navy blue business suit and a crisp white blouse, navy heels with white dots around the edges. Her clothes alone would make her glamorous to me, but her glamour is everywhere. Her fingernails are shaped and polished, showing off the large jade rings and diamonds on each hand. There are pearl earrings in her ears and a string of pearls around her neck. Her hair is pure white, and has been since she was in her twenties, although sometimes she arrives with it tinted blue or lavender; always it is expertly curled and coifed in an upswept style.

She wears high heels and perfume and rouge and eye make-up. Red lipstick smudges the ends of her white filtered menthol cigarettes in the ashtray by her side. I love the deep dimple that appears on her lower left cheek when she smiles, and I love her liquid brown eyes and throaty laugh. Aunt Lorraine loves to laugh, and gets everyone else laughing. She has so many things to talk about that the conversation never ends.

Priscilla, still in her robe and slippers, looks at Aunt Lorraine as happily as everyone else. This woman is so magical and yet so genuine even Priscilla is drawn to her. Every time she visits, Aunt Lorraine brings expensive house gifts or something elegant for Priscilla to wear, while also coming prepared to pull out her own needlework and join Priscilla on the couch for some time sharing craft projects and techniques. At night, while Aunt Lorraine sips the scotch she brings along, she will get our somber Dad laughing and singing away at the piano while she thumps out popular tunes in a jazzy style. For him she always brings a crazy toy from F.A.O. Schwartz that they wind up and watch careen around the living room floor. They are cousins, and as close as brother and sister, although she can only get here for a visit once or twice a year.

I'm trying and failing to hide my stuffy nose. Aunt Lorraine, overlooking it, says, "How about I pick you up after school and we'll go for a ride."

"Okay," I say happily.

"Sounds like you've got yourself a nice juicy head cold," says Priscilla dully. "Shouldn't you be in bed?"

"No. It's nothing. I'll be fine," I say as I clear my dishes from the table, and damn it if the Christian Science or the power of positive thinking or some such thing doesn't kick in right then and take that cold away before I make it upstairs to gather my books and papers together for school. I stand looking at myself in the mirror over my bureau, tilting my once leaden head this way and that, testing each nostril. Not a sign; not a single sniffle. Gone. I twist my lips into a lopsided sneer, almost getting a dimple to appear in my lower left cheek.

School that day is a challenge. School is always a challenge, making the weakest of penetrations through the murk of my psyche. But on this day of all days, when I can think of nothing else but going for a ride with Aunt Lorraine, Mrs. Milliken decides she must keep me after school and force me to catch up on my geography workbook. She has never before kept me after school. She sits at her desk correcting papers while I try and try to focus on the overwhelming number of blank pages in the workbook. It's not that I don't know the answers, but who can concentrate when Aunt Lorraine's car has been sitting at the gateway to the schoolyard since the bell rang? I keep going up to the teacher's desk to show her my work, all the while craning my neck to make sure Aunt Lorraine's car stays there and she doesn't give up on me.

Mrs. Milliken asks, "Why do you keep looking out the window?"

"That's my Aunt Lorraine's car. She's visiting. She was going to take me for a ride after school."

Mrs. Milliken gets assigned to a higher cloud in heaven that day. She takes pity on me, immediately telling me I can take the workbook home. I race as fast as I can out of the building and across the playground.

Suddenly I notice Grammie sitting in the back seat. My feet slow. As I open the door and say hi, Aunt Lorraine says casually, "Your Grammie wanted to come along for the ride. Hop in the front seat with me, Sweetie." As the car pulls away from the curb she asks, "So how come you were late?" When I explain, she says, "Well, then. We'll keep our ride short and get you home so you have plenty of time to do your school work."

Just because this woman has a huge heart and seems to keep it filled with enough love for everyone on the planet doesn't mean she is a softie. Aunt Lorraine is a business woman who owns her own company in Greenwich, Connecticut. In the mid 1950's, that makes her remarkable. She flies all over the country to meet with clients, and is used to letting people know her mind. She doesn't put up with nonsense, even from me.

Once we are back at the house, Aunt Lorraine asks me to show her the workbook and the work I have to do. Then she instructs me firmly but lovingly to go up to my room, do the work, and come down and go over it with her when it's done. Sitting on the edge of my bed, I work hard to fill in all the answers to questions like, "Name three rivers in North America," and "Describe the climate of the desert." I use my best handwriting, too. I want Aunt Lorraine to be proud of me.

Snuggling next to each other on the couch, we go page by page through the workbook. For one answer, I have called upon my favorite word from the movie "The King and I," which we recently took Grammie to see at the drive-in. "Etcetera, etcetera, etcetera!" Saying that the way Yul Brynner said it delights me. So when the workbook question asks for a list of crops grown in the south, I write "cotton, etc."

Aunt Lorraine asks, "Do you know what that word means?"

"It says, 'and so on, and so on, and so forth,' like he says in the King and I when Anna is teaching him the word. It means there's more." Aunt Lorraine explains that it's not a good way to answer a workbook question. I need to let the teacher know what I know. She sends me back upstairs to work on that one some more.

While I'm still working on my answer, I hear Aunt Lorraine coming up the stairs. This is a surprise. I've never known her to come upstairs. She sleeps in the living room, where the couch opens up into a bed. "Where are you?" she sing-songs from the top of the stairs.

Sitting down next to me on the drab army cot with the four square bedposts she takes a long look at the wallpaper: the plaid, the masculine athletes. Putting her arm around me, she says quietly, "I took your mother and grandmother out for a nice long lunch in town today. And then we drove around to look at all the spring flowers and bushes in bloom. I thought that would take care of everything, but when I was leaving to pick you up after school, your grandmother said she wanted to come along for the ride. I'm sorry, Sweetie. I wanted some time just for the two of us but it didn't work out that way. I wanted you to know it wasn't my idea." The hugging arm gets another firm grip on my shoulder and holds me close.

Aunt Lorraine spots my postcard collection stuck into the frame around the mirror on my bureau. "You like postcards?" she asks. I show her each one and talk about how it all started with a postcard I wrote to Grammie on a weekend drive to Vermont. Somehow the card never got mailed. "I'm going to start sending you postcards," Aunt Lorraine says. "Would you like that? My travels take me all around the country, so I'll send you one from each place I go. But I want you to promise that you'll write to me, too. Will you send me letters and let me know how you are and what you are doing?"

Should I tell her that Priscilla and Dad read every letter and card that their children write, so they can check the spelling and grammar and approve of what we say? Should I tell her they read every card and letter I get in the mail? I decide to let that go. She probably knows that will happen if we correspond. "It would be fun to get your postcards," I tell her. "I promise I'll write. I'll write to you lots and lots."

Aunt Lorraine gets up and takes a peek in the other bedrooms before she goes back downstairs.

It's almost bedtime. When the phone rings, I can tell it's Aunt Lorraine calling by the happiness in Dad's voice. They josh around for a while, then all I hear is, "Uh-huh. Uh-huh." Aunt Lorraine must have a lot to say. Dad, standing in the hallway, pokes his head around the living room archway and says to Priscilla. "Can you come here, Honey? Lorraine wants to talk to you, too." A little bit of warm up, a little bit of sweet talk, and then Priscilla is mostly listening, saying "I see," now and then.

When she is done, Dad calls me downstairs. "Susan. Aunt Lorraine wants to have a word with you." This is the first time in my life I have been called to the phone, so I sit a little awkwardly on the straight-backed chair placed by the phone table in the hallway, trying to figure out the best way to be comfortable with that big, black receiver in my hand.

Aunt Lorraine wastes no time. "Listen, Sweetie. Don't say anything back to me, just listen, Okay? I know your mother and father are right there in the living room and can hear everything you say. I've just told them that I am shipping a bed up to them that I want you to have. It was my bed when I was a girl and it has just been sitting in storage. Don't say a word now because this has to be between you and me, but that's just plain wrong the way they've got you in that room with that wallpaper. I've made it very clear to them that I want the bed to go to you."

"Uh-huh," I say, in the spirit of a secret-keeper. "That sounds good." I run out of ways to cover up the real subject matter, so I say, "Thank you, Aunt Lorraine. I'll write you a letter soon," We say good night and hang up. I head upstairs wordlessly, disappearing before anyone can see the grin on my face.

I don't understand why Aunt Lorraine wants me to have a different bed when it's the wallpaper that is so out of place. But by the end of that call I do understand one thing: I have an ally. And I have secret knowledge that my parents' decision to keep that manly wallpaper on the walls does not sit well with other adults – at least this one very special adult. I am no longer alone in thinking it's a constant insult to me. In the larger picture of mistreatment, it's not much, but it is something I can hold onto.

The day the bed arrives, the movers carry it up the stairs, put it together, and take the old cot up to the attic for Priscilla. She is beside herself with spite when I get home from school and follows me up to my room. "I don't know why you should have a bed like this, Your Royal Highness. When was the last time you did anything to deserve something like that?" But there is nothing she can do about it, and that galls her.

I can't believe my eyes. It's gorgeous. The bed frame is dark cherry wood, polished to a high gleam. The headboard has an open weave carved into it and a scrolled rounded top. The footboard has a wide flat top that is perfect for sitting on the bottom edge of the mattress and resting my feet as I look out the front window. It is two mattresses high, the bottom one a box spring. And it is covered with the most beautiful dusky rose satin bedspread, quilted and fitted precisely to the bed, with skirts to the floor. A very girlie bed. For me.

Aunt Lorraine calls again that night to make sure that the bed is there, in my room, and that the movers took care of everything the way Priscilla wanted them to. I don't get to talk to her this time, but I am working on a very carefully worded thank you letter.

Before Aunt Lorraine returns for her next visit, Priscilla finds a scatter rug to match the bedspread. She buys matching fabric and makes satiny dusky rose café curtains for both of the windows in my room. She scolds me angrily for making scuff marks on the bedspread when I forget to take my shoes off before resting my feet on the footboard. She takes to referring to me as "Her Royal Highness" or "Miss High and Mighty" or "Her Nibs" in front of the rest of the family.

"Before you start thinking too much of yourself, Your Nibs," Priscilla says, snapping shades down and pushing the new soft curtains across their rods as I carefully fold back the satin bedspread and climb under the covers, "just because your Aunt Loraine wants to spoil you, you'd better remember what I've told you a hundred times before. Until you start doing as you're told around here, you have no right to anything. You've done nothing to warrant anything from anybody. You just can't seem to learn that, can you? I have no use for you." She marches out and shuts the door roughly.

All of this is witnessed by the golfers and the football linebackers and the baseball batters, their presence unchanging no matter how incongruous each successive dusky rose improvement looks against the red plaid backdrop.

The Sound of Silence

Pricilla has no scruples about being mean to me in public, in front of anyone and everyone – relatives, neighbors; children, adults. No one openly faults her for the way she is behaving, so my sorry lot is always on display. In the privacy of our home, Grammie is there, giving Priscilla her whole-hearted support. Dad never speaks against Priscilla, and would consider it outlandishly disrespectful to say anything critical about his mother-in-law. So there I am, in a community of people who act as if Priscilla is doing nothing wrong. Which means I must be doing something wrong. Which means Priscilla has a right to be vindictive about my very presence because I've totally messed up being a daughter and a member of this family.

Sometimes I feel a deep sadness as I brood about trying to live through the rest of my childhood and adolescence. Clearly I will get no help from Dad, who lives in his Christian Science world where all is good and perfect. He expects his children to do the same. To his way of thinking, we three kids should appreciate having a strong, healthy mother who can sew our clothes and keep our house and cook our meals – and who does all that with talent and proficiency. Even if Dad were capable of seeing any of Priscilla's behavior as unconscionable – for a mother or for any responsible adult – he would burrow deeply into his Christian Science brain and do the mental work required to remove that imperfect idea and restore the all-goodness of his universe.

He has already fallen into the habit of seeing Priscilla's manner with me as a matter of my own failure to think all-loving thoughts and to practice the religion he has given me. In other words, the problems are all in my head. Besides, he's in this so deep now he can't go back. He can't undo his years of faith in Priscilla's all-goodness in order to retrieve situations that he never should have allowed to happen. He can't de-escalate what has been ratcheting up day by day right in front of his eyes, while he played the silent bystander. He can't switch gears and begin to play an active role in mediating her behavior. He is now, has always been, her devoted husband. As time goes by, he has less and less of a relationship with me because I'm not there to relate to. I'm in my room. He probably pictures me there, practicing my Christian Science thinking.

He also has two children who are daily reminders of what a good mother Priscilla is. Penny and Stephen are having decent childhoods, except for being forced to live with a pariah in the family. As long as they block out the fact of my existence, which is easy to do when I am kept out of sight, they can enjoy a pleasant family life. They have a mother who behaves like a mother to them and both they and she seem to need to keep it that way. All indications are that if they try to question the way I am treated, put in a word for me or take my side on anything, they will jeopardize their own positions in the family. They see me for breakfast and supper; days and weeks go by with no other times of being in the same room. Normalcy for my siblings is to emulate their father and witness without question my treatment at Priscilla's hands. Over time, they will stop seeing Priscilla as the source of the problem and come to believe that I deserve to be treated the way my mother treats me. It's the only explanation.

Every world I inhabit – home, school, neighborhood, church – is full of children who take their mother's love for granted. There are no other children out there like me, in the situation I am in with Priscilla. I know this because I am always checking. I ask other kids about their mothers and other mothers they know. I probe when they have complaints about their mothers, wanting to know exactly how other mothers behave when there's a problem. When we're driving through the Boston suburbs to visit relatives and friends on the weekends, I am peering in all the houses we go by, wondering if any other child out there is going through this. But I have never met one who is. Consequently, I carry the shame and guilt of knowing I am the only one in the world so unworthy that I do not deserve the mother love that everyone else comes by naturally.

The love I long for is talked about in Sunday School. It is in the words of the Bible and in The Science and Health with Key to the Scriptures, both of which I read daily in order to complete the church-assigned readings every week. Dad insists on this. Usually the word Love is capitalized, to show its enormity, its god-like quality. But for me, Love remains elusive, something I apprehend in odd bits and snatches, those fleeting moments when the fog in my mind clears enough for me to consider the existence of that spiritual force Mary Baker Eddy refers to as omniscient, omnipresent and omnipotent.

One song in particular in the Christian Science Hymnal penetrates my sorrow and despair. It's my favorite hymn. I wish we sang it every Sunday:

Hymn #207

O gentle presence, peace and joy and power
O Life divine, that owns each waiting hour,
Thou Love that guards the nestling's faltering flight!
Keep Thou my child on upward wing tonight.

Love is our refuge; only with mine eye
Can I behold the snare, the pit, the fall:
His habitation high is here, and nigh,
His arm encircles me, and mine, and all.

O make me glad for every scalding tear,
For hope deferred, ingratitude, disdain!
Wait, and love more for every hate, and fear
No ill – since God is good, and loss is gain.

Beneath the shadow of his mighty wing;
In that sweet secret of the narrow way,
Seeking and finding, with the angels sing:
"Lo, I am with you always," – watch and pray.

No snare, no fowler, pestilence or pain;
No night drops down upon the troubled breast,
When heaven's aftersmile earth's teardrops gain,
And mother finds her home and heav'nly rest.

Grammie sits and tats lace doilies and knits fine sweaters, leaving little balls of chewed gum in the empty ashtrays around the house. She claims that chewing gum helps to remove the sensation of always having hairs at the back of her throat. She and Priscilla are in the sunroom when I come home from school, knitting and chatting, probably devising more and more mean ways to quash that evil spirit of mine. I call out the expected, "Hi," as I pass through the dining room on my way upstairs, but neither one responds.

Dad's away. He has received frequent promotions and raises at the CH Sprague Coal and Oil Company in Boston, sometimes two or three times a year. His latest position as comptroller requires him to travel all the way up the Maine coast, once in the fall and once in the spring, stopping at the company's satellite offices along the way to audit their books for tax preparation. He is gone for a week each time.

I change my clothes and go over to play in the schoolyard with my friends. Within minutes I hear Priscilla call me. It's still early, much earlier than she usually calls me to come home. Penny and Stephen are out somewhere. As I come in the back door to the kitchen Priscilla says angrily, "Haven't I told you to come when you're called? Didn't I tell you to stay where I could see you?" I am positive I was within sight and heard her on the first call, so I nod yes in confusion. "Go up to your room," she says. She follows me upstairs with a thick wooden plank about four feet long. She tells me to bare my bottom and bend over the bed. She swings that board way up in the air and brings it down hard to spank my behind, over and over. "If you don't start doing as you're told I will spank you with this board so hard you won't be able to sit down for a week. Do you understand me? Now go down and talk to your grandmother."

I go downstairs and stand in front of Grammie's chair with my head bowed and the tears flowing. She keeps tatting. The sound of her clacking false teeth chewing gum keeps time with the clacking needles, filling the silence. Without looking at me she asks, "So have you learned your lesson? I would think by now you would have learned to obey your mother. I hope you're ready to pay attention to what she says. Go up to your room and think about that."

The board spankings happen again and again, only when no one else but Grammie is home. The reason for it always strikes me as manufactured, as if Priscilla so relishes the opportunity she just has to get that spanking out of her system. I am sure that Priscilla does not tell Dad about it. The plank stays out of sight, amid the coats and boots in the hall closet. Whenever she feels like it Priscilla says, "Do you want me to get the board?" One time she says it at the dinner table in front of Dad. He looks up, puzzled, but lets it go.

The board, and the injustice of her using it for no reason, marks the end of the days when I take all of the blame for my situation onto myself. I am beginning, at least partially, to believe that I am a victim of something dark in Priscilla. I am sure that if I could talk about it with someone outside the family, they would want very much to come to my rescue. But where would I begin? How could I describe my oppression and isolation, which is a total greater than the sum of its parts? No single event or behavior, no cluster of images I might convey could even begin to describe what I live with day after day. Who would I tell? And if I did, what would happen to me? The minute Priscilla, or Dad for that matter, finds out that I have complained about her, I am positive I will be punished beyond the strength I have to endure.

It has taken me months of hiding from Priscilla's eyes – in Ruthie's driveway, which is three houses down from us – to finally get my sense of balance and ride a bike with confidence, using one or another of the old beat up two-wheelers in Ruthie's cellar. Ruthie doesn't mind at all if I come over to play with her and end up spending most of the time by myself, sneaking in practice on how to ride a bike. It's an accomplishment I have to keep from my family, since Priscilla has forbidden me to ride anyone's bike.

Ruthie is an amazing friend, the second oldest in a family of four girls. Penny is friends with the oldest one; they go off and do things that teenage girls do, like looking at Seventeen Magazine and trying out hair styles on each other. Meanwhile, Ruthie is like my personal camp counselor. She has a limitless supply of sports and hobbies to interest me. She has taught me how to play tennis, both the moves with the racket and the rules of the game. She is teaching me archery with a bull's eye target that her father set up in her back yard; we use real bows and arrows. She has introduced me to horseshoes and badminton and ping pong and a lot of jump rope moves. She can press wildflowers, make lanyards and run a sewing machine as well as a grown woman.

The hardest part of my friendship with Ruthie is that her family goes to their place in the Berkshires for the entire summer. It is so lonesome without her. Most of the other kids are gone, too; their families have places on the Cape or up in Maine. I walk down to the town playground a lot, where teen-aged leaders get ball games and craft projects going, the same ones day after day The most exciting days there are when the kids spot muskrats in the adjacent Aberjona River; they're fun to watch.

I'm getting to know a girl my age named Mara, a city girl whose grandmother lives in the house across the street from us. Mara just appears one day each summer, sitting with her younger brother on the curb across the street. Her parents, college teachers who work in the summers, bring their kids up to their grandmother's in Winchester so they can have a summer vacation away from New York City. Once Mara shows up at the bottom of her driveway, I have someone to be with every day for a month or so. Most days we play canasta, talking for hours as we sit on the bed in her room. Her grandmother likes us to be quiet, and I know all about that.

Since my mother has been reviling me all of my conscious life, it's a wonder to me that Ruthie, Mara or any other child wants to be around me. What could anyone possibly see in me? I am so guarded and emotionally beaten down that any personality I may have had is hidden in some deep recess somewhere. I expect to be shunned and outright rejected. When someone acts like a friend, I hold back and shrug it off for a long time; I need to be sure, take nothing for granted.

Even though I know my aunts and uncles care for me, I expect other adults to look at me with disgust, to find my presence unworthy of their attention. They see me treated as the lowest of the low by the woman who is supposed to have the greatest familiarity with my character;

it's as plain as the nose on their faces that I'm someone they shouldn't bother with. It comes as a surprise, then, when Mrs. Davis next door calls my mother out of the blue one day and asks if I can come over. Priscilla acquiesces with a reluctant, "I suppose so."

Mrs. Davis, Molly, seems elderly to me, even though her son Stuart is my age. Her hair is iron gray, short and tightly curled. She doesn't smile, which to me means she's either sad all the time or upset about something. The thought of spending time with Mrs. Davis scares me. She seems to live in the shadows inside her house, rarely visible as a full-blown person in the light of day outdoors. I hardly ever run into her and when I do, she is difficult to talk to. Stuart goes to private school now, so I only see him once in a while; he is the only topic of conversation we ever had.

She opens the door – a tall, thin woman in a gray dress and low heels, holding a cigarette, arms crossed – and gives me her spooky version of a smile. It lifts the corners of her mouth a little but doesn't touch her brown eyes. The interior of the house is dark and musty smelling. She leads me through to a sunroom, where she has spread out materials from a craft set for making mosaics. As she teaches me how to do a mosaic piece, she says, "I always wished I'd had a daughter. I'd love to have you visit. Now that Stuart's away all day, it's pretty quiet around here. You can come over as often as you like, Susan." Before I go she shows me a bookshelf full of Stuart's books, and, being an avid reader, I succumb to the invitation to take as many home as I want, "as long as you return them."

I can tell that she is subtly probing me here and there for information about my situation at home. Anyone who is around our family for even a few minutes would have to be deaf, dumb and blind to miss Priscilla's animosity towards me. I suspect that Mrs. Davis has spied on us from one of her bedrooms; my bedroom is directly across the driveway that separates our houses. I've seen her in an upstairs window sometimes, trying to hide back in the shadows. Did she witness some board spankings? She could probably see that board going up and down, over and over. Still, instinct tells me to deflect the neighbor's curiosity. When I return home Priscilla asks, "What did Mrs. Davis want?"

"Nothing," I say. "We did mosaic tiles. She misses Stuart and let me take some of his books to read. She wants me to come over every Wednesday."

Mrs. Davis teaches me a different craft on each visit. I learn how to make beaded trinkets and how to fashion copper jewelry with a little soldering iron. After a few weeks, she asks my mother for permission to drive me to a rehearsal of the community theater production of A Midsummer Night's Dream. I love watching the action on stage, long to be part of it. I just read a biography of Sarah Bernhardt in school and my dream is to become an actress. I must have let something of that slip to Mrs. Davis. But when Mrs. Davis points out all of the children on stage and asks me if I am interested in joining the theater, I say no. The reality is, I just can't imagine Priscilla being willing to make my costumes and find me rides to and from rehearsals. After that, to my relief, poor, sad Mrs. Davis stops trying.

Soon afterward, Mrs. Ball takes a crack at it. Mr. and Mrs. Ball live in the house after Stuart's, the one just before Ruthie's. They are an older couple with a grown son who lives in another state. Mr. Ball is a banker who wears wire-rimmed spectacles and is built like my Dad, tall and beefy. His name is Ed, too. Mrs. Ball, Millie, is plump and dresses well, with an apron over her skirt most of the time. She wears heels, make up and jewelry every day. She has an exaggerated way of saying some vowels: the "u" in Susan makes it sound like Sewsan. My parents call it a Brooklyn accent. This couple has tried to be good neighbors since the day we moved in – bringing over a catalpa tree to plant in our back yard, having our whole family over for Christmas visits and stopping by on the weekends for backyard chats.

One afternoon Mrs. Ball is out gardening and sees me playing by myself in the back yard. "Oh, Sewsan," she trills. "Do you want to come over and help me do some weeding?"

I go inside to ask Priscilla. "Oh, I suppose so," she says.

Mrs. Ball shows me how to use her weeding tools and I carefully weed alongside her as she probes for information about my life in the family. There is little subtlety to Mrs. Ball, so the conversation is a challenge for me.

"Hasn't your mother taught you how to weed? She's got a lot of gardens over there."

"Well, she likes to do it herself."

"I bet. So how are you doing?"

"Fine."

"What do you do at home?"

"Oh, I read. I play viola."

"How are things with your mother?"

"OK."

I am positive that more harm will come to me if I start blabbing to a neighbor about what a horrible mother Priscilla is. Instead, I talk about how hard Priscilla is working to take care of Grammie. Eventually, Mrs. Ball lets it drop, but she takes me inside for a glass of lemonade, gives me $2.00 for my help, and tells me I can come to her house any time, even if all I want is a glass of lemonade. "I'd love to have you visit, Sewsan" she says. "Just come over anytime."

"What did Mrs. Ball want?" Priscilla asks when I get home from weeding.

"I helped her weed and she gave me $2.00," I say. Then I sit on the back steps in the sun for an hour, pretending to read a book but contemplating how far away I can get on those two dollars. Where can I get a bus? How far could it take me? What if I walked down to the train station and went to Boston? Then what would I do? I could try to see Dad in his office, tell him what goes on when he's not around. No. Absolutely not. He wouldn't believe me, or he'd defend Priscilla's right to do whatever she wants to do. Where else could I go? How many times would I have to weed with Mrs. Ball to get completely away?

For the rest of my days on Marshall Road, all through junior high and high school, Mrs. Ball watches for me coming home from school once or twice a week. She stands in her front doorway, holding the door open, and saying in her Brooklyn accent, "Oh, Sewsan. Yew look just like Grace Kelly." The smile on her face is warm and friendly. She asks how I am, how school's going and what's new. She asks if I can come in for a visit. Every time I see her in her doorway my nerves jangle with stress. I'm torn between wanting to be polite to this nice lady and knowing that any delay in my arrival time at home is going to incur the wrath of Priscilla.

But the real lesson of Mrs. Davis and Mrs. Ball is the sure knowledge that I can tell no one what I am going through. No matter how I play it out in my mind, "telling" just isn't going to work for me. I am stuck in a caricature of the nuclear family of the 1950's, where the mother stays at home and takes care of the children and the household while the father goes to work. To all outward appearances, my family is living the American Dream. We live in a very fine house on a quiet tree-lined street in one of the wealthiest suburbs of Boston. I am receiving an outstanding education in one of the top three school districts in the state. Thanks to Dad's regular promotions in a large corporation, we are upwardly mobile, have all of the material goods we want, and can afford leisure experiences like vacations at the beach. In this era, parents have a right to raise their children as they see fit, and no outsider has a right to assail the walls of that fortress with questions and criticism. I suspect Mrs. Davis and Mrs. Ball come to the same conclusion.

I am walking up the sidewalk to the house. The insistent hum of a machine starts to follow me, slowly growing louder and louder. It's the scissors grinder, I realize, coming down the street on his little cart, powered by the motor from a lawn mower. It goes so slowly a crawling baby could outrun it. When he is in the area, he rings the bell attached to a pole by his steering wheel to let housewives up and down the street know that he is here in case they have things that need to be sharpened. The back of his cart bristles with knives, saw blades, scissors and tools to show customers all the different things he can sharpen with his grinding wheel.

Something's odd about the sound of the scissors grinder's cart. It sounds menacing. Is it coming for me? Oh, my God, it is! It's coming after me! And the scissors grinder is out of the cart and chasing me with a pair of scissors almost as tall as I am! I am running, running to make it to the house and get away from him, but he is right behind me. Never run so hard in my life. Can't catch my breath. Run, Susan, run! I race inside the house. Slam the door shut behind me. Did it lock? It must have locked. Take the stairs to my room two at a time. I can't breathe! I can't breathe! I fling myself on my bed. Oh, no! I hear him coming up the stairs!

I need to scream! I have to be able to scream. "Help!" I am trying to scream. "Help!" But nothing comes out. I can't speak. I have no voice. My throat and tongue are paralyzed. I keep trying. "Help!" Nothing. No sound. I strain my throat with all my might, trying to get that scream out. He is in the doorway! He is kneeling over me on the bed, one knee on either side of my legs, the long scissors blades wide open and coming for my throat! He's going to kill me!

I make one last heroic effort to scream "Help. Help." Although I still cannot produce a sound, the effort at last wakes me up from this nightmare. My pajamas and the sheets are soaked with sweat. My heart is beating like a tom-tom inside my chest. The house is still. I made no sound. I had no voice.

Exile

The old maple table on the screen porch is elongated with two leaves, clothed in a red-checked tablecloth and covered with an assortment of picnic glasses and plates, bowls of pickles and chips, bottles of ginger ale and pitchers of lemonade. The grill is fired up. Metal TV trays have been unfolded and scattered around. Because of the extra chairs and lamps placed out here for the occasion, the space looks homier than it does when we do a family supper on the porch.

Grammie's whole family is at our house for a cookout. Besides us, we have her younger daughter, my Auntie Belle, and Auntie Belle's son, my cousin Donnie. Then there's Grammie's son, my Uncle Bud, and his wife, my Aunt Wilma, and their two children, my cousins Lynn and Greg.

I am awkward around my cousins for several reasons. The obvious one is that they have mothers who love them and I don't. Their visits put me on display as the only unloved child in an extended family of six children. At ten years old, I also fall between the age groups. Lynn, Donnie and Penny are all around twelve years old; Stephen and Greg are five.

The penal code I have to follow every time they come for a visit doesn't help matters either. Since I can't come downstairs until Priscilla calls me down, I don't get to greet the arrival of company. Sometimes she doesn't call for quite a while. When she does utter that, "Susan," from the bottom of the stairs, it's a lifeless name, dropped grudgingly from her jaws like a cat being forced to give up a dead bird it would much rather play with for a while.

A couple of times I've sat in my room and never been called to take part in a visit, as if I didn't exist. That hasn't ever happened when it's the aunts and uncles visiting though. They wouldn't stand for that, I know. But I also know that sometimes Priscilla pretends she already called me down and I just didn't hear it. As if I wouldn't be listening for the cue to join the group! Two can play that game. One time I had the moxie to stay put after my name thudded like lead balloon against the stairwell. I stayed absolutely still, made not a sound. Made her call me again, I did! But the second, "Susan!!" spat out like an angry epithet, was all I needed to give up my brief rebellion.

In any event, it's hard to get too deeply involved in what the cousins are doing because at some point Priscilla is going to march right up to us wherever we are playing, arms akimbo, hands on her apron and say, "Susan. Go to your room." There won't be any reason for it. It will just be something she feels a need to do.

When that happens, I use the hubbub of voices below as cover for sneaking a book out of the bookcases that line the hallway upstairs. Those shelves are filled with best-selling novels Dad and Priscilla get every month from the People's Book Club. I hide one at a time under my mattress. The remaining books I jostle into a loose formation so no one can tell there's one missing. There's an Encyclopedia Britannica set in its own special bookcase, too. I long to harbor each one of those for a while, but I don't dare. There's no good way to hide the blank spot that would be left in the set.

Tonight has felt different from the start. Why, on a warm July night, did Priscilla instruct me to change out of my shorts and put on jeans and a sweater? All I can imagine is that she expects this celebration of Grammie's 70th birthday to go on for a while, into the cool of the night. And then, she called me to come down and sit on the screen porch before anyone arrived! This is unheard of. It's my favorite place in the whole house and she never lets me sit out here. I'm musing about all this while I absorb the earthy blend of the day's humidity and the evening's shade coming out of the piney woods across the street. The lawn outside burns with that jeweled green tone that intensifies as the sun's long summer rays collapse against the ground.

The olives and chips are so tempting I finally get up the courage to help myself. Greg and Stephen have jumped on opposite ends of the glider and are pumping it as hard as they can, getting it going so fast its metal feet thump against the wooden porch floor as they giggle hysterically. Donnie and Lynn are out in the back yard playing catch with the ball and glove he brought. Out in the kitchen, Aunt Wilma's booming voice weaves over and through the little girl voices Auntie Belle and Priscilla get when they're together. Dad and Uncle Bud come out to the porch, reviewing the features of the big charcoal grille as Dad gets to work on grilling hot dogs, hamburgers and buns. Penny, Auntie Belle and Aunt Wilma take turns bringing out platters of potato salad, macaroni salad and devilled eggs. Pitchers of iced tea appear on the table, and a crockery pot of homemade baked beans – Grammie's favorite. She likes to make cold bean sandwiches with the leftovers.

When it's time to eat, the women go to Grammie's room to persuade her to come out to the porch. She has been feeling poorly today and has not yet joined the party. "I'm too queasy," she tells them. "You go ahead. I'll rest and try to join you later."

As we all sit around eating our picnic supper, I am eavesdropping on the adult conversations I so rarely get to hear. Dad explains the awnings – broad-striped and scalloped-edged – newly installed around the porch. They have handles that winch them up and down. Dad's spirits lift like those awnings when he gets to play the jovial host and forget about his incessant search for a positive path through my experiences with Priscilla. He smiles and laughs more when company is here.

Priscilla fields questions about the differences between philodendrons and the rhododendrons growing along the front of the porch. She's knowledgeable about gardens, has several blooming out back. She seems at ease as she sits in a straight-backed chair, her legs crossed at the ankles, knees together, arms folded under her ample bosoms and wedged into the waistline her apron strings help to identify. She has on a short-sleeved pink-checked cotton dress, one of three she made recently from the same pattern.

I do love being out on the porch. I wish I could come here after school to do homework, or on the weekends to read. Screen porch cookouts are one of the best parts of summers in this house. The evening light and soft summer breezes are starting to make me all gooey with beatitude. On top of that, I'm such a pushover for any signs of softening on Priscilla's part that I find myself relaxing tonight because she let me come down here early and she hasn't been after me all night. I fantasize that her tyranny is over. "Now that Grammie is sick a lot," I tell myself, "Priscilla doesn't have time to pick apart every little thing I do."

Uncle Bud has a deep, gruff voice. "That's my niece, Susan, over there. Isn't that right, Susan." It sounds like he's mad, but he has this goofy grin on his face that lets you know he's joking around. "I need to talk to my niece, Susan, for a while. Come here and give your Uncle Bud a hug. How's everything goin' for you, kid? OK?"

"Ya," I say, shy about his big love coming my way.

"You're gettin' tall," he says, wrapping me in one of his bear hugs. "You're all skin and bones there, girl. How're we going to fatten you up?" I shrug my shoulders, trying to imagine a world where Priscilla has no authority so I can eat like a normal kid. "Aw," he says. "That's a good girl. We got chemistry, right? Me and my niece Susan got chemistry. Isn't that right, Susan. Yes, that's right," he answers himself.

"Let's see how Mummer is feeling," says Priscilla. Uncle Bud unravels his arms from me and goes with his sisters to peek in on their mother, see if they can persuade her to come out to the porch for birthday cake and ice cream. Pretty soon Uncle Bud comes back, walking slowly through the living room with Grammie on his arm, escorting her out to the porch with his two sisters close behind.

The shrinking process has begun. Grammie looks shorter and less bulky than she did just a few weeks ago, before she went into the hospital for an operation. Since then she hasn't always come to the dining table for dinner. In fact, I've hardly seen her since she came home. When did she decide she will no longer get dressed each day? She's in her bathrobe and slippers, her hair matted down in the back. Looks like she got out of bed for this. Grammie smiles around at the crowd.

"Watch the step down, Mummer," Priscilla says.

"Here, Mummer. Sit here," Auntie Belle says, standing by a chair near the door.

"Move the table closer to that chair, Honey, so she can reach things,"

Priscilla says to Dad. He pulls the card table that is piled with Grammie's birthday cards and presents over to the chair.

Grammie looks up and around at all the people gathered on the porch and enters into light-hearted teasing with the grown-ups about her age. Priscilla goes to the kitchen to put candles on the special cake she made with Grammie's favorite light meringue frosting.

"OK, Mummer?" Uncle Bud says. "Are you doin' OK? Can you sit right there where Belle is?" He helps her into the chair.

"I'll get the afghan for your legs, Mummer," says Auntie Belle.

Priscilla enters with the cake lit up and we sing Happy Birthday to Grammie. She has a big smile. "It's your favorite, Mummer," Priscilla says. "The white cake with the whipped frosting." She has decorated it with delicate pink roses. She and Grammie admire it, their heads bent together over the cake. It is, as usual, picture perfect, a masterpiece of a cake.

Soft lighting has begun to separate the porch from the brightly lit living room and from the deepening India ink outside. Priscilla shoots me an occasional sour look, but has not reprimanded me for a single transgression. Not only have I escaped the usual solitary confinement, but I am being allowed to stay up well past my bedtime – something else to puzzle over. I think, "Maybe it's because this could be the last time Grammie will be able to have a party."

Despite her ill health, Grammie loves being the center of attention and perks up under the glow of everyone's concern for her as she opens her presents and nibbles some cake. Eventually she tires, and her faithful daughter Priscilla takes her back to bed and helps her settle in for the night.

The rest of the crowd starts picking up, traipsing back and forth from porch to kitchen, where Auntie Belle and Aunt Wilma have taken over the clean-up. I am wallowing in la-la land, imagining a new life with Priscilla, one without the meanness. I've made it through this event as much like a regular member of the family as I've ever been, and it feels good.

When it's time to say good-by to Auntie Belle and Donnie, I stand in the front hallway with everyone else, giving hugs. I'm tired. It's 10 PM, and I am ready and willing to call it a night. We start saying our good-byes to Uncle Bud and his family. Priscilla abruptly says, "Susan. Go upstairs to your room. There's a suitcase on your bed. Bring it down here. You're going with your Uncle Bud to see how it feels to live on the other side of the tracks."

These are the first words Priscilla has addressed to me all night. I can only stare at her, dumbfounded, in return. "Hurry up," she says. "They need to get going. Don't make them stand around waiting for you all night."

A small suitcase sits open on my bed. Open, so that I can see two new outfits of shorts and shirts folded carefully on top of the other clothes. I stand there fingering a new white jersey with a plaid collar, pleased with Priscilla for doing at least that. No doubt it's meant to entice me into going with Uncle Bud without putting up a fuss. It's so like Priscilla, to manufacture evidence of what a good mother she is to me, while doing something awful to me at the same time. It's her way of proving that I'm the one who willfully persists in misreading her intentions, making her out to be a nasty person. If I balk, I will be shown to be an ingrate in this script already written to laud Priscilla's generous spirit.

Suddenly I understand the night. I understand why I had to dress in jeans and a sweater, why I was called down to the screen porch before anyone came, why I've been allowed to stay up so late. The suitcase tells a tale of premeditation. Priscilla spent the night and more time beforehand arranging this moment. The entire evening has been staged.

I close the latches. The weight of sadness and shame descends from my head to my toes, so much heavier now in the aftermath of what I took to be a mellow night. I take the suitcase by the handle and drag myself down the hallway to the stairs, where all those faces are looking up at me. Only Uncle Bud is looking at the floor, deeply hurt by Priscilla's demeaning comment about the other side of the tracks. The faces of his entire family look bewildered by this turn of events. I thought they must have all been in on it, but the faces say no. They had no idea. I wonder if Dad knew. I look at him sadly, but his face gives away nothing. I can't even look at Penny and Stephen.

"You say good night to your father," Priscilla says crossly. Dad and I exchange a wordless kiss on the cheek.

If I ask the questions to which I need answers right now – like why and for how long – I know I'll just get into more trouble for speaking up. It will be taken as "talking back to your mother." It's bad enough to be abruptly sent away, as if one of my recent sins was so awful my presence can no longer be tolerated under the same roof as the rest of the family. I should know by now that these things have no rational basis, but my mind is racing anyway, searching for clues. The only hint I have is that bit about seeing what life is like "on the other side of the tracks." Maybe this has something to do with not appreciating the material goods my parents provide for me.

My loyalties are in utter confusion. I mean, I love Uncle Bud and his family. They love me in return, which is nice to be around. I know they'll treat me far better than Priscilla does. I have new clothes I'll be happy to wear. But I didn't want to say good-bye to my father. I don't want to start a new life at the age of 10 in someone else's family, no matter how awful my situation is. I don't want to have to deal with all this uncertainty about what is going on.

In the darkness of Uncle Bud's car, as we drive away, five-year-old Gregory asks over and over again, "Why is she going to our house? What's she going to do?"

I listen carefully to the words Aunt Wilma chooses. "She's just coming for a little visit, Greg."

"She'll just be staying with us for a while, Greg."

"We'll just have her with us for a few days and she'll do with us everything we usually do, Greg."

"But why is she living with us? Where will she sleep? What is she going to do? Why is she coming to our house?" Greg's most repetitive questions echo in all of our brains.

Uncle Bud drives fast and smooth through late night traffic squirting on and off the southbound lanes. Wedged between Lynn and Greg in the backseat, I watch familiar exit signs go by: the one to the dentist in Boston, the one to the Christian Science Mother Church, the one to Uncle Ralph's in Quincy. "Are you watchin', Lynn?" Uncle Bud asks his daughter. "You're gonna be drivin' soon so take a tip from your old man. When you're on the highway, drop your speed just a whisker under what the cars up ahead are doin', then sit back and watch the highway in front you open up. See that? Beau-tee-ful."

"Uh-huh," says Lynn in her soft-spoken manner.

Greg is asleep, his head nestled into the corner. I'm starting to notice all the rips in the old station wagon's upholstery, the dog hairs and the choking odor of my aunt and uncle's cigarette smoke. As we leave the Cape-bound highway to jag inland on back roads, tiny pricks of light poke holes in the thick darkness. "What *is* that?" I ask, pushing up to the edge of my seat so I can see through more of the windshield.

"Fireflies." says Aunt Wilma.

"Wow!"

"You never saw a firefly before?" Lynn asks.

"No," I say. "I read about them though. There's so many! That's really neat."

The drive through rural Berkley finally ends with a turn onto Point Street, a rutted dirt road that parallels the Taunton River – which flows into Fall River, which flows into Narragansett Bay. The familiar tarpaper shack jumps into the headlights, a rusted cistern on its sagging porch. Sally the collie prances around the car, barking joyfully. When I get out, she sniffs me all over, as confused as the rest of the family about what I'm doing here. While Uncle Bud gets my suitcase out of the back of the car, I follow the others inside.

One open room inside goes from a kitchen area with its round dining table, to a living area with a sagging couch and chair, both covered loosely in faded print sheets, to bunk beds set against the far wall. It's cramped and jumbled and about the size of the screen porch on Marshall Road. Aunt Wilma and Uncle Bud set up a folding cot as a bed for me and place it perpendicular to the bunk beds, where Lynn and Greg sleep. The only other rooms in the house are a tiny bathroom and a bedroom off of the kitchen.

I lay awake, listening to the voices of Uncle Bud and Aunt Wilma talking quietly in their room behind the closed door. Sally's nails tap-tap against the linoleum floor. Deep into the night Greg calls out huskily in his sleep, "Did you get me the pail, Lynn?"

The days that follow bring many lessons from the other side of the tracks. For example, Aunt Wilma has an old wringer washing machine for her laundry. She has to hook a hose up to the sink to fill it and then she hand cranks the clothes through the wringer. She is happy with this arrangement because not too long ago she was washing all of their clothes by hand. Still, given the effort involved, clothes do not get tossed into a laundry hamper after a single wearing. Aunt Wilma tells me, "That is not how it's done here. You need to wear things a few times, let 'em get dirty. I'll tell you when they're ready for a wash."

When it's time to get ready for bed, Uncle Bud has to teach me how to "wash up" using a basin in the kitchen sink – a procedure that takes the place of baths and showers. The three of us kids take turns washing up. Uncle Bud watches me to make sure I'm doing a good job and reminds me if I forget to do my neck or ears or feet. We don't wear pajamas to bed either. As far as Uncle Bud is concerned, pajamas are unnecessary. You go to bed in your underwear. Well, Lynn is wearing bras these days so she gets to wear a big T-shirt to bed.

Uncle Bud is a metal worker at the Reed and Barton Silver Company. He is also a first-rate auto mechanic. About a hundred yards down the gently sloped yard, where his property meets the river, he has a garage where he works on the old clunkers his friends and neighbors need to keep in working condition. In the evenings and on the weekends much of his time is spent down at the garage, earning a few extra dollars being a mechanic. Some of his customers pay him in fresh vegetables from their gardens.

One day when I walk down to the garage with him after supper he stops to pick up a bolt he finds in the grass. "Don't leave anythin' like that lyin' around, Susan," he says. "You see a nail or anythin', you pick it up and save it for your Uncle Bud. Nothin' goes to waste around here. If somethin' breaks, you fix it. You find somethin', you put it to use."

To one side of the shack is a hill of dirt that Gregory loves to climb up and pee off of while singing "The Wayward Wind" at the top of his lungs. That pile represents hours of Uncle Bud's labor to clear a spot on his property where he can build a house for his family. He has an ancient tractor he has fixed up to use with different attachments to help him remove boulders and stumps and dig a foundation. He is doing all of the design work for the house himself. It is going to be sited so that a big living room window looks out on the Taunton River below.

Aunt Wilma takes Lynn and Greg and me blueberry picking down where the dirt road ends and the wild blueberry bushes are loaded with fruit. She teaches me how to tell which berries are ready for picking, and how to remove the stems. Our buckets are tin cans with strings looped through holes punched at the top. She expects us to fill them up so that she has enough berries to use in her cooking this week and then plenty more for freezing. We go blueberry picking three days in a row to get the job done.

Auntie Belle and Donnie come down from nearby Randolph to visit on Sunday afternoon. Uncle Bud parks the tractor in the middle of the cleared land, produces a can of red paint and several brushes, and lets all four of us kids paint the tractor. We paint the wheels, the fenders, the engine hood – everything in sight. Not once does Uncle Bud tell us we're doing it wrong or criticize the drips going everywhere. One by one, he lets us sit up on the big metal seat, tells us patiently how to drive a tractor, and lets us take it for a ride around the property. He's such a good teacher it feels like the easiest thing in the world to be doing.

Lynn and I spend a hot afternoon walking to her friend's houses – far apart on those rural roads. We cross huge open fields, gather friends to hang out with, and end up in a deliciously cool horse barn where Lynn flirts with a boy they call "Flat Top" because of his haircut. The two year's difference between Lynn and me seems huge.

Time After Time

I am discovering that it's OK to be a kid here. Kids can do lots of things without being constantly scolded. Although Uncle Bud and Aunt Wilma don't hesitate to offer corrections or instructions, they aren't after kids all the time. They do use their big voices to make a point, and at first that scares me. At home I use Priscilla's spiteful tone and cranked up volume as measures of how serious my offenses are. But when Aunt Wilma childes me with a gruff, "Did you forget to brush your hair this morning?" she does it with a little grin. "Can't go 'round here lookin' like a wild woman, you know, just cuz we live in the country. Go get that brush, Susan, and do your hair. That's a good girl."

I never see them spank their kids. In fact, anyone can tell they love their children to pieces. It's in their eyes when they look at them, and in their voices and affectionate gestures when there's a shared moment. Adults and children talk to each other! They have conversations! There's too much laughter and delight in one another to dwell on their economic difficulties. Their love is as large as Aunt Wilma's tall, raw-boned body and Uncle Bud's barrel chest.

I'm the odd ball because I'm quiet and don't know what to say. I'm not used to being openly affectionate, or openly anything for that matter. I know I'm intruding. I know my manners. I'm just trying to be a good guest in their lives. But I also get the idea that Uncle Bud and Aunt Wilma think I am too guarded for a child and need to loosen up, experience some freedom for a change.

After supper the next Saturday, Uncle Bud says, "It's time to call my sister Pete. Isn't that right, Susan. Ah, yes, that's right, Uncle Bud. Come and sit here while I call and talk to Pete." I've been here over a week and no one from my family has called. He takes the easy chair by the phone table and I sit across from him on the couch, next to Aunt Wilma. Lynn and Greg are playing down at the water's edge.

"At least there's a plan," I think to myself. "Maybe this was just for a week and now I can go home." Uncle Bud is asking his sister if she and Dad will come down to get me tomorrow or if he needs to drive me back to Winchester.

My uncle and I are practically toe-to-toe in the cramped space. I'm watching his face as he listens to Priscilla and grunts monosyllabic answers while staring at the floor. He looks up at me and lifts the receiver a little ways away from his ear. In a strangely quiet way he says, "Susan. Would you like to stay here with your Uncle Bud another week or go to your Auntie Belle's?"

The option to go home is missing from those words. I don't want to hurt Uncle Bud's feelings, though, so I try to hide the disappointment and say to him, "I'll stay with you."

Uncle Bud relays my answer quietly to Priscilla. "Would you like to speak with your daughter?" he asks her. The answer is obvious as he hangs up the phone.

"Penny and Stephen got the mumps," he says to no one in particular. Then, seeing my tears, he keeps talking quietly. "If you went home, you'd get the mumps, too. Your mother doesn't want another sick child on top of the other two and taking care of Grammie. Sounds like your grandmother has been very sick. So you'll stay with us, isn't that right, Susan. Ah, yes, that's right, Uncle Bud," he answers himself with a valiant grin as he keeps his eyes on me. "Come over here and give your Uncle Bud a hug. She's a good gir-rul, that Susan. We got chemistry. My niece and me got chemistry, isn't that right, Susan. Some got it. Some don't."

As his affection soothes me, I think, "Well, at least I know it's only for another week." But at the end of that week, Uncle Bud and his family drive me over to Auntie Belle's in nearby Randolph. If I had known the plan meant I had to stay with Auntie Belle regardless of the amount of time I'd been at Uncle Bud's, I would have chosen to go to Auntie Belle's last week – get my exile over and done with.

Auntie Belle and Donnie live in the second floor apartment of a house in Randolph, just a couple of blocks from the downtown area. "Belle's Alterations," says the wooden sign swinging on a post out by the street. The constant noise of street traffic contrasts sharply with the near wilderness of Uncle Bud's place, but the apartment seems spacious and full of light after two weeks in a tiny, dim shack.

Time After Time

Auntie Belle is a seamstress. This particular week she is creating eight royal blue taffeta gowns for a bridal party. The dresses hang in similar stages of completion in her living room, on a large rolling rack that also contains pants, skirts and other articles of clothing she has taken in for mending and alteration. Her dressmaker's dummy stands in a corner of the dining room. She uses her dining table to lay cloth flat when she needs to cut out a pattern.

People come to Auntie Belle's all week for fittings and to pick up clothes. She works and works and works, all day and into the night. She works on the weekend days. What is she supposed to do with me? She's used to having her older sister Pete boss her and Uncle Bud around, though, so when Pete tells them the least they can do is take me off her hands for a while given all the work she's doing to care for their mother, there's no room for argument. Auntie Belle borrows a fold-out cot from a friend and sticks it in her bedroom so I can sleep in there. It's a good thing for her that I've become very quiet with this shuffling from place to place. She can get her work done even though she's got an extra child around to take care of.

Donnie is unhappy about having a girl around, especially a younger girl. His mother is so busy earning a living that he is used to coming and going as he pleases. If he could have someone to pal around with he would have a rough-and-tumble guy like himself, or someone like our cousin Lynn – on the threshold of adolescence, capable of pitching a fast baseball and willing to sneak cigarettes behind the corner store. "You throw like a girl," he says in disgust when I try to give him a little batting practice out in the front yard after supper.

Donnie is a pudgy, freckled redhead with a chip on his shoulder that comes from losing his father four years ago. One day Donnie came home from school with a cold and the next thing he knew his father got pneumonia and died. He blames himself for Uncle Jimmy's death. Auntie Belle doesn't talk about Uncle Jimmy much anymore. Her face is very sad, though, and she has a chronic spasm in her neck that makes her head twitch to one side, over and over. "Is that because you have to bend your head over your work all day?" I ask her.

"Oh. No," she says with a sigh. "It started when my Jimmy died." The nervous tic gets worse at the end of the day when she is tired.

One day she sends me off with a neighborhood family, complete strangers to me, for an afternoon trip to a nearby summer fair, giving me a quarter to spend and a dime to call in an emergency. The only thing I see at the fair that I want is a little toy dog that squeaks when you press his belly. It costs thirty cents, so I spend some of my emergency dime. Back at the apartment, I sneak into Auntie Belle's bureau drawer where she keeps her change, and swap my remaining nickel for a dime that she has there.

When she asks for her emergency dime back, I am ready, and pull it out of my pocket. But Auntie Belle suspects me of foul play immediately, because she knows she had a dime left in her drawer, and now it is gone. "Did you take the dime that was in there?" she asks.

"No," I lie. I hate lying to her. I hate it that I took her money. I hate it that she and Uncle Bud are so poor and my family has so much. Maybe this is the lesson Priscilla wanted me to have: I am leading a life of privilege. Other people have to work and work and work for every dime. They don't have TVs and washing machines and cookouts on the porch. So what if my mother treats me like a criminal? Look at all the advantages my parents have given me! Look at the hardships other people live with! You should be grateful! Anyway, now I know I have to cross the relatives off my list of possible runaway destinations because they couldn't afford to take me in.

Auntie Belle tries to talk Donnie into paying me some attention one morning. Before we can do anything, though, she has to send him to the corner store for a loaf of bread and some peanut butter; the cupboard is bare, the refrigerator empty, because she hasn't gone grocery shopping. She doesn't have a car. A trip to the supermarket in a neighbor's borrowed car takes more time that she has had this week.

When Donnie gets back, he decides to take me fishing with a simple line of red twine wrapped around a palm-sized square of wood. To Donnie's surprise and mine, I catch six horn pout with his crude fishing device, pulling fish in frequently enough to keep us at the pond for hours, fishing and nibbling on peanut butter sandwiches like good ol' buddies. I make Donnie do everything that has to do with touching the worms or the fish, though; I'm too squeamish.

While we are gone, Auntie Belle sews patches on the knees of my jeans, because they are worn and she sees that it needs to be done. She should have taught me how to do it for myself, she's so busy. With Auntie Belle as my teacher this week, I have finally learned how to baste a seam, sew on buttons, mend holes in my socks and do a chain stitch and a back stitch for hems.

"You're homesick, aren't you, Dear," Auntie Belle says as I watch her work one day.

"What does that mean?" I ask her. I don't think I've heard the word before. She tells me it's a feeling that comes from missing your home. "Oh," I say with a shrug. "I guess so." I'm not sure what I feel.

When Saturday rolls around, Auntie Belle tells me that my parents are coming to get me. Suddenly I am glued to the couch by the front window so I can watch for the car. "It's way too early, Dear. They won't be here until after lunch," she says.

I am homesick. I feel it now. I miss everyone in my family, but I am surprised by the realization that I miss Priscilla most of all. I am so used to having every waking hour occupied with her expectations and her criticisms. "Maybe this is what she meant about seeing what it feels like to live on the other side of the tracks," I muse. "That a three-week absence from her would make my heart hurt so bad I would look forward to going home. That being away for a while would make me appreciate having her for a mother. That's crazy. Do I really want to go back and live with her way of treating me?"

I begin to wish I could grow up really fast, right there on Auntie Belle's couch, so I would know how to deal with going home. At this moment I would happily trade off spending the rest of my childhood with a tender mother in a loving family for a chance to remain part of the family I have, even if the part I play continues to be that of the loathsome intruder. I don't understand why I feel that way, after all these years of wanting to escape, but that's the way I feel.

I wonder what Priscilla has thought about me. Have I been far enough away for long enough to make her miss me just a little? Has she changed her attitude towards me? Does she feel any excitement today about coming to get me? The possibility of going back to a Priscilla who has the exact same reactions to my presence that she's always had is too painful to imagine. I decide to pin my hopes on time as a healer. It has to have made a difference, being away this long, because now the slate is wiped clean. For three weeks I haven't done anything to offend Priscilla and Priscilla hasn't done anything to wound me, so we can start over.

"They're here!" I shout to Auntie Belle when I see the green Pontiac pull up at the curb below. I hurl myself off the couch, out the apartment door and down the stairs. The minute I open the front door I see Priscilla right there, halfway up the sidewalk coming towards me.

"Hi, Mummy!" I say, smiling from ear to ear as I run to her and fling my arms as far around her waist as they can go. I hug her tight, my head on her bosom. Priscilla puts one of her arms tentatively around my shoulders while the other holds her pocketbook by its handle down at her side. Briefly, oh, so briefly, she gives me a hint of a squeeze in response. In that moment, what I wish with all my heart is to know the woman who did that. I want her to be my mother – not the Priscilla I deal with, not Aunt Wilma, not Auntie Belle.

"Well!" she says, as if surprised herself by the strength of our greeting. I can feel her slipping back into the old Priscilla. "So! Have you learned how to behave yourself? Are you going to be a good girl now?" Those are typical Priscilla questions, but I promised myself I would be meek and obedient no matter what. I drop my arms, look my mother in the eye, and say softly,

"Yes."

"See that you do," Priscilla responds as she heads inside.

I reach for my Dad, who has been looking upon the scene between his wife and his middle child the way a field hand looks upon the Promised Land. I understand, as he does not, that the only healing that will come out of the past three weeks has already happened, right there on the sidewalk. We will go home. Priscilla will continue to treat me the way she has always treated me. We will all have to live with that until I am old enough to leave home. Eight more years to go.

For many days and nights, however, I can recapture the feel of that hug. I had a few seconds of benevolent contact with the warm body that belongs to my mother. I can recall the feel of her arm around my shoulder and across my back. I can relive that hint of responsiveness from the hand attached to that arm. I know that in that moment she was not repulsed. She liked the fierceness of my homesick arms around her waist. It made her glad that I was happy to see her. She wasn't expecting that. These are all drops of comfort I squeeze from the memory until it is bone dry.

Points Of Departure

On the Brink

On good days, days when I'm managing to hold onto the ragged hem of self-esteem, I try loving Priscilla fiercely all day, no matter what she does. "She will be compelled to love me back," I tell myself. "I can make the force of my love so strong she'll feel it." It is within my power to do this. The only religion I know expects me to be able to do this. If all that's needed is a strong will, steely discipline and a backbone, that "good, stiff spine" the grownups talk about all the time, I have plenty of all that.

Here I am, scared out of my wits by Priscilla, but I don't hate her. She is my mother and I am always and forever thinking about how to turn this situation around so that at last I'll know her love.

Looking at her across the breakfast table, I project my love. I project God's Love. I consciously reject the intrusion of any negative feelings. In my mind I'm listing over and over all of the good things Dad or Penny or Stephen would say about her, good things I would say about her.

"She's a wonderful cook."

"She does such beautiful hand work."

"She knits sweaters for me."

"She sets my hair in curlers for Easter Sunday."

"She works hard to keep the house clean, wash and iron our clothes, cook our meals."

"Every year she fills the dining table with all kinds of Christmas cookies she's made, then gives boxes of them to the milkman, postman, bakery truck driver, S.S. Pierce delivery guy, the neighbors, the relatives and people Dad works with."

Again later, while I eat my lunch, I go through the list again. Then I mentally rehearse compliments like, "Thank you for the delicious lunch. I really like tuna fish," or, "That cream cheese and olive was delicious." I do this whenever it's not baloney and cheese on buttered bread or peanut butter and jelly. Once in a while she'll make peanut butter and banana or peanut butter and bacon sandwiches. I compliment her on those, too. I know she won't respond, but I make an effort anyway.

If it's after school, though, I try to stay under her radar when I come home. I can barely get out the "Hi, Mum," that is required for the sake of politeness. She doesn't feel like "Mum" to me but there is nothing else I can call her. I practice the word in my head as I walk down the sidewalk and up the back stairs to the kitchen, knowing she won't welcome the sound of my voice or the fact that I am home. One of these days I'm going to succeed at making myself invisible as I come through that door.

For now, though, I have to steel myself to run the gauntlet from the back entryway where we leave our coats and boots, through the kitchen, down the hallway and up the stairs. I hope for the best; that is, I hope Priscilla will thoroughly ignore me. If she is not in the kitchen I go through the dining room so I can see if there is any mail for me, which would be left propped up against a candle holder on the hutch. I get an occasional postcard or letter from Aunt Lorraine; each one makes her love for me real and helps me live with Priscilla's tyranny.

If Grammie is feeling well, she and Priscilla will be sitting in Grammie's room when I get home, knitting together companionably. They are silent as I pass by; neither one saying hello in response to my greeting. Even when they are engaged in making something for me to wear they ignore me. Recently they started knitting a skirt and sweater set for me out of rust colored boucle, a yarn that they keep telling people is dreadful to work with. Priscilla comes to my room time and time again to measure both me and the evolving outfit, saying repeatedly, "I don't know where you get those hips of yours, Your Highness. Must be all the sitting around you do, doing nothing." The comment makes me feel tubby, even though I'm thin as a rail.

She won't be knitting with Grammie on Tuesdays and Thursdays; those are ironing days. Priscilla is right there in the kitchen when I get home, half-hidden by that tall drying rack she uses to hang ironed clothes on. I try to make my body disappear when I go by so I can slip past the pointed end of the ironing board without getting attacked. She slaps that iron down on the board like she's just itching to brand my hide.

If she says nothing to me as I pass through on my way upstairs, I've still got to stay on high alert until Dad comes home. The sound of Priscilla's loafers leaving the linoleum floor in the kitchen, clicking sharply against the bare wood in the hallway then heavily against the oriental runner, coming up the carpeted stairs: those are the dreaded danger signals. Not again! Watch out! Red alert! Scramble! Extreme danger! Find something so you look busy, Susan! Quick!

Lately it seems like she's on a one-a-day plan, thinking up something that causes her to come at me in a fury every single day. If I don't get it on my way through the kitchen, the rampage begins within minutes of my coming home, after I'm in my room and have barely finished changing my clothes. God help me if she finds me sitting around thinking about things, when she's so busy all the time. Being idle would ignite a tantrum the size of Kansas.

"You left a ring in the bathtub, Your Highness." Malice makes her voice coarse and heavy. "I asked you if you cleaned up after yourself in there and you lied to me. Didn't you? Answer me! Didn't you?" My emotionally overloaded, muddled brain slows my response to what Priscilla is saying, which makes me feel stupid. I search for answers to her questions that will save me, but I come up empty. Puddin'-headed Susan. "I shouldn't have to tell you again. You get on your knees and scrub that out. Put some effort into it, instead of being so lazy! I'm not going to do it for you. That tub better be spotless when I look at it. Helpless, hopeless, useless."

"It's high time you did something else besides sitting around all day. Now get out there and shovel back those snow banks from the sides of the driveway. Your father shouldn't have to do everything around here just because you're too lazy to lift a finger. I had better not catch you resting on your shovel out there. Try earning your keep for a change."

"Didn't I tell you to pick up all of the apples in the yard so your father can mow? Didn't I? Have you done that yet today? Are you going to tell me there aren't any apples on the ground out there? Are you? No. You sit there doing nothing. As usual. I've told you over and over to get out there and do your job. I shouldn't have to tell you again. I'm fed up with you. Helpless, hopeless, useless. Now get out there and do as you're told. Think about other people for a change."

"Just how did your socks get so filthy, Your Nibs? Huh? What do you have to say for yourself, huh? What were you doing, huh? What do you do, walk to school in your stocking feet? I wouldn't put it past you. I'm fed up with this. I am not washing anything that you get so filthy. You're going to wash them yourself. See if that teaches you a lesson. You get down cellar right now and scrub those in the set tubs with the bar of Fells Naptha down there. I don't want to see a speck of dirt on them when you're done."

I sleep on sheets that have a seam up the middle, because Priscilla says I am too lazy to cut my toenails and that's why the worn sheets she gives me to put on my bed get rips in them. "It's not enough that I have to cook meals for you and pick up after you. Now I have to sew your sheets, too? I don't have time for this. If you would cut your toenails the way you've been told time after time this wouldn't have happened, would it? Would it? What do you have to say for yourself, huh? You haven't got the sense you were born with. You can just put those sheets right back on your bed, Your Highness. You'll be sleeping on them from here on. Serves you right."

A button is missing from my coat, my blouse has an ink stain, a zipper's broken, a sock has worn at the heel, a skirt hem has ripped. "Just look at that! You're to fix that," whatever the item of the day is, "instead of assuming other people have nothing better to do than to pick up after you all the time. I'm sick and tired of your carelessness. I've told you time after time to take care of your things. Do you have any idea what it costs your father to keep you clothed?"

While she grabs me hard enough by the upper arm to leave a ring of black and blue tracks, or while she flings the offending article across the room at me, she berates my scurrilous being in general as well as my latest offense in particular. The force of her rancor brings tears to my eyes.

These are the only words she exchanges with me in the course of a day. No greetings or good-byes, no inquiries about my experiences, thoughts or feelings. To make eye contact with her is to meet a look full of loathing and spite.

Of course, part of the problem is my utter inability to predict what will cause her fury, which means I have no way to stave it off. It shouldn't be such a grievous sin that buttons come loose and apples fall to the ground. But in Priscilla's mind, anything that displeases her or disrupts the perfection she is trying to maintain is my fault, something I have deliberately done to offend her. For that I must be punished. We cannot discuss it like reasonable people. I cannot question why it makes her so mad, or examine the truthfulness of her accusations; I must accept the blame and correct the problem to her satisfaction.

Now that I have grown taller than Priscilla, I've taken to standing up when I hear her approach, hoping that my height will give me an advantage of some kind. At least if I stand she'll have to reach up to grab my arm or yank my hair. However, my whole body starts to tremble when I hear her coming. It's an internal, invisible shaking, like a taut wire vibration that thrums through every nerve, blood vessel and tendon. Fear turns my legs to jelly. The minute she leaves I have to sit to help the tension ratchet back down. One of these days my body is going to decompose right in front of her eyes, unable to bear that extreme stress any longer.

I rarely feel hunger any more, might forget food altogether if I didn't get called to the table. Getting to sleep at night takes a while, and staying asleep until morning hasn't happened since before I went to Uncle Bud's. My ears are becoming bionic, they work so hard to gather information for me, information I use to figure out what the family is up to so I live in less of a vacuum, information I need to stay on guard against Priscilla.

I have lost the ability to urinate if Priscilla is nearby. She started following me upstairs after I go down to say good night. She sits in the chair in the hallway, outside the bathroom, waiting, while I am in the bathroom peeing and brushing my teeth before bed. I don't know why; all she is waiting to do is close my shades and shut my door without saying a word, which she continues to do like some parody of the dutiful mother tucking her child into bed. Sometimes she calls out, "Get a move on, Susan. I haven't got all night." Knowing she's sitting there, about four feet from the door, causes my bladder muscles to freeze shut.

Now, any time she is around, in the hallway or in any room upstairs, my muscles refuse to let go, no matter how badly I need to relieve myself. Needing to go in the middle of the night is the worst. Her head is on the pillow right behind the bathroom wall where the toilet is. When I can't stand the discomfort anymore and make myself get up, it takes forever, sitting there, trying to make my body let go.

My brain also freezes when Priscilla's near. The pathways of thought are gluey, gummed up with the glop of primal fear. It takes months for a glimmer of reason to get through and suggest that if I brushed my teeth and peed before going downstairs to say good night, that would be a good way to work around this problem.

"Aren't you going to brush your teeth?" she asks, the first night I change the sequence and go upstairs and right to my room instead of the bathroom, with her on my heels.

"I did it before I went downstairs," I said.

"Huh," she grunts.

But it's too late. Even at school now, I can't pee in the girl's room when others are in there. This has become a chronic, painful situation that causes me to sneak around, behave oddly, desperate for the privacy I need. As far as I can tell, no one else suffers from this condition so it's one more thing to be ashamed of. I'm a freak.

At least Priscilla can't follow me inside my head. In there, I am able to look at her behavior and know that what she is doing to me is wrong and mean and sick. With my mind's eye I can look at myself humanely, and try to grasp that what she thinks of me and says about me has no basis in reality. Deep inside I cultivate the belief that I am a good person, worthy of her respect and love.

I brood, though, up there in my room, trying to find a way out of or around any of the hundreds of obstacles Priscilla has set up against my having a normal life. Lately it seems like I cry every day. I cry as I review the situations of the day or the past few weeks. I cry because the way she treats me hurts like the dickens. I cry because remembering one thing and everything hurts me all over again. I cry because everyone in the world can pee when they want to and I can't. She's taken even that away.

Sometimes I entertain myself with images of how Priscilla might suddenly die. Or I try to imagine a disaster that I alone would survive – maybe a flood or a tornado. Then Aunt Lorraine would take me away from here forever. If something like that doesn't happen, I won't be able to have a life until I'm all grown up.

But real life intrudes the moment I hear Priscilla coming. I grab a book or a pad of paper to promote the appearance of industry, while my legs quiver like little sticks of gelatin. My skin pales. My scalp prickles. My heart goes running up a mountainside. A torrent of blood rushes through my ears. My breathing seems to stop altogether. Across my chest and back, down my limbs and inside my skull, the neural pathways become racecourses where conflicting signals careen crazily around the curves and crash into each other. My tongue and throat feel like they're stuck in a bale of cotton wrapped in barbed wire. If I am forced to respond to Priscilla's attack, my voice wobbles out on a stream of air so thin the words fall over in a dead faint, refusing to assemble themselves into upright columns of thought. Even if her destination is somewhere other than my room, just to hear her coming sends my body into this state of preparedness for extreme peril. It stays like that until she returns to the ground floor.

This is not a boisterous family, but these days everyone tip-toes around trying to muffle every little sound. Conversation at the dinner table is as hushed as if we are sitting in pews. While we are eating, Priscilla has an ear cocked to her mother's room, right behind my chair. At some point during the meal she will hear something worrisome, get up, go into Grammie's room, come out carrying a small, clear plastic container with an inch of violent orange liquid in the bottom, go to the bathroom off the hallway to flush the fluid away, wash the dish, return it to Grammie, check to see that she has quieted again, then come back to the table. All the while the rest of us eat slowly, chew quietly, keep our eyes on our plates.

Grammie has cancer. The doctor comes to see her regularly. Occasionally, while we three kids are at school, an ambulance comes and whisks her away. She endures another operation, gets more treatments, recovers a little. Dad murmurs to us across the dinner table, "Grammie came home today so you three kids keep your voices down." The relentless process of getting sicker and sicker attacks her again, until it's time for the next hospitalization.

Dad makes a potty for her room. He removes the cane bottom of an old chair, fits a basin in there and gives the wood parts a fresh coat of white paint. "Ooh, Eddie! You made me a white Cadillac," Grammie says. "Look at that! I get to sit in my very own white Cadillac!"

The biggest role we three kids play in these events is that of sentry: sitting on the spare dining chair outside Grammie's closed door while Priscilla is getting meals ready, so that we can report any little sound of distress that goes on behind the wall and let Priscilla know right away. Even I get called out of my room and pressed into sentry duty at suppertime, if Penny is out babysitting and Stephen is playing at a friend's house.

"Susan." Sharply spoken, but not too loud. "You get yourself down here. Right now." As I come down the stairs, "You sit by your grandmother's door there and listen." She snaps her fingers while pointing down at the chair, her eyes downcast, her forehead pinched with stress. "Come get me immediately if you hear anything." I sit still as a stone and will Grammie not to make a sound so I don't have to get Priscilla, who goes about making the noises she has to make to get supper ready, knowing a spare pair of ears is tuned in for her.

The only time I might see Grammie is after breakfast, when Priscilla walks her to the bathroom for her morning wash-up, if Grammie's well enough to do that. I've seen enough to know she is wasting away, like a plump potato that is being pared and pared and pared.

The toll this is taking is obvious. Priscilla is gray with fatigue. Mild-mannered Dad is so concerned for his wife he occasionally gets cross with us out of the blue. "You three kids need to be doing more for your mother! Don't wait for us to tell you what to do! See what needs to be done and take care of it!" He is utterly frustrated by not being able to make this ordeal disappear into the mists of Christian Science perfection. He would give his soul to alleviate Priscilla's burden with positive thinking. "Your mother has enough on her hands right now! You three kids need to be helping out more around here!"

There's not much else we could do. Penny and I are already alternating weeks of being responsible for either dusting or vacuuming the house, and alternating days of either clearing the table or doing the dishes. I am responsible for dusting and polishing the bannister on the main staircase and for keeping the cellar stairs clean every week. Penny has always been welcome in the kitchen, so she is able help with meal preparations. We make our own beds and clean our own rooms.

Stephen's main job has been to go to school and "stay out of your mother's hair," as Dad puts it. But my brother hates school so much that he cries every morning.

"I have a headache," he pleads as he wilts in the downstairs hallway, waiting for Priscilla to take pity on him. He's not ready for school but he knows he's not welcome at home when he should be in school.

"I'm not going to put up with any nonsense from you on this subject," Priscilla tells him sternly, bustling him into his jacket and sending him out the door in tears every morning. The school has told her she needs to teach him how to put on his own snow pants and mittens and boots and coats, but she has babied him for so long he doesn't understand this sudden pressure to do things for himself.

I pass by his classroom one day when my class is coming in from recess. Stephen is standing at his desk, all alone and crying. His snow pants are on, but the rest of his winter gear is piled in a heap on his desk. With permission from my teacher, I go in to see him, put my arm around his shoulders. His sweaty jersey testifies to prolonged sobbing and standing around half-dressed for the outdoors. Those saucer eyes sprout new tears as his little fingers pull at the suspenders on his snow pants. "What's wrong?" I ask.

"I have a headache," he wails.

"Do you want to go home?" I ask.

"I can't," he sobs. "The teacher says I can't."

He's probably tried that headache ploy too many times. Looks like his teacher has narrowed his choices: get yourself dressed or stay indoors. I have to leave him there like that, knowing I can't help, knowing how it feels to be powerless to make something awful turn out good.

I am drying the breakfast dishes I just washed, putting them away. School's out for the summer. Today is my twelfth birthday. One of those quintessential June days is waiting for me outside, all sparkly with effervescent sunlight falling through the dancing leaves.

Here comes Grammie, leaning on Priscilla's arm to make her way to the bathroom. Her quilted aqua bathrobe billows around her. She pauses to contemplate how to shuffle across the threshold between the dining room and the kitchen without losing her balance. "Hi, Grammie," I say, pleased to see her despite the shock of her appearance. She is so very, very tiny now, like a little bird.

I am surprised when Grammie smiles a toothless smile at me and grunts back. She can't speak much anymore. "Mmmufgh!" she exclaims in her excitement at seeing me there in the kitchen. "Grrng. Mmmgh." Brief but enthusiastic grunts I can't make out, each one causing her free arm to scribble a message in the air. The sudden movement makes her lurch into Priscilla; that fragile body so easily topples.

"She wants to kiss you happy birthday," Priscilla says with disgust.

I can't believe my ears. I put down the dish towel, walk over to bend down and give Grammie a very gentle hug. She smiles at me the whole time and kisses me on the cheek. I kiss her soft, soft cheek in return and say, "Thank you, Grammie," with my biggest, warmest, happiest smile, looking right into her eyes.

The fact that I'm having a birthday brings no joy to anyone else; it's a grim ritual to get through at the dinner table. Penny gets her favorite checkerboard cake every year, Stephen gets his chocolate, and they both get a lot of good-natured teasing about their birthdays, from the breakfast table until bedtime. We three kids make a fuss over our parents' birthdays, too, because we know that's the customary way to behave, acknowledging in ways both silly and loving the importance of someone's birth. Nevertheless, when it's my birthday, no one smiles and jokes with me; no one asks ahead of time if I want anything in particular. I've made a game out of waiting to see how long into the day each person goes before managing to mumble an unsmiling "happy birthday" in my general direction.

Priscilla never says it. She begrudgingly makes whatever cake she feels like making and I am lucky that she allows me to have a slice for dessert. One time she made brownies. When my face betrayed my dismay at the sight of them, she said. "What's the matter? I thought you liked brownies. That's what you always order for dessert when we go out to eat."

Tonight, a brochure is by my plate at the dinner table, along with the birthday cards and presents. "Take that up to your room after supper and read it. Do what it tells you to do," Priscilla says. "I haven't got time to chase after you and see that you're doing what needs to be done. Talk to your sister if you can't figure it out for yourself. You're to be ready to leave after breakfast on Monday. The bus will pick you up at the Main Street entrance to the school playground." Dad, as usual, says nothing.

This is how I learn I am about to attend the Harvard-Newton Summer School. My heart sinks at the idea of going to school for eight weeks out of the summer. Just what I don't need – more school. But I know Priscilla doesn't want me hanging around the house; Grammie's care is her primary concern.

The brochure tells me that this is a special enrichment program, offering students who are about to enter junior high a chance to experience ahead of time what school will be like at the junior high level. Students select the courses they want, have classes with different teachers and change from one classroom to another during the day. Class size is kept small. I've been signed up for courses in English and geometry in the morning. In the afternoons everyone participates in writing and art. I'll need pencils, a ruler, a protractor, a pencil compass and a pad of paper. We're supposed to bring a pocket dictionary. A lunch period includes a break for swimming at a nearby public park. For that I'll need a suit, a bathing cap and a towel, as well as a lunch.

That's a lot to get ready. I ask Penny if she has a protractor and compass I can borrow. She cleans out her dark green cloth book bag with the dingy yellow canvas straps that draw it to a close and hands that over as well. I find a couple of decent pencils in my drawer, a pen and a pad of paper. The night before classes begin, I go downstairs to ask Priscilla which towel I can take, and she asks Penny to get me a certain one from the linen closet. I finally get my bathing things packed, and my things for class. In the morning, I take the brown lunch bag that has been placed by my plate, add it to the bulging book bag, and walk across the playground to wait for the bus. No one says good-bye or have a good day or hope you like it.

I've never been on a school bus. This should feel like an adventure. The book bag is awkward and heavy, so I rest it on the sidewalk by my feet as I wait, thinking about how Priscilla needs me to be out of her sight. She must be thrilled that she found a way to do that for the whole summer. Lately she can't even be bothered to call me downstairs for meals. She sends Penny or Stephen to do it. I find that really insulting.

I groan inwardly again at the thought of trying to focus on geometry and English classes. At least they let you wear shorts and sneakers; you don't have to dress like you're going to school. A yellow school bus comes around the rotary a block to my left. It pulls up in front of me.

As I walk up the steps into the bus, the book bag bumping against my leg, I hear a voice call out, "Susan!" Looking down the aisle of seats, I see a hand waving at me and walk towards it.

"Hope!" I exclaim when I get near enough to recognize her. "Oh my gosh! Are you going to this school, too?" My best friend from Prince Ave, whom I haven't seen since we moved and who now looks exactly like a miniature version of her mother, looks at me quizzically.

"Didn't your parents tell you?" she asks. "My parents told me you were going. They thought it would be nice for us to see each other again. Did you know we're going to see each other in school from here on? We'll be in junior high together, too."

Hope is a fountain of information. More importantly, I have a friend to go through this experience with, even though as we chat, we realize we are taking different courses. What a treat to be with Hope again! "This summer school thing is going to be O-K," I think, as the school bus pulls into a shaded circular drive in front of a red brick school in Newton.

At the dinner table that night I can barely wait to spring my surprise. When Dad asks me how the program was, I tell him excitedly, "Hope was on the bus! She's going to this school, too!"

"We know," says Dad evenly. "We ran into her parents in the 5 & 10 one Saturday and they told us." Is that why they signed me up? Wouldn't you think they'd tell me something like that? I can't for the life of me figure out how these people think. I'll never know. Dad is all done talking about it. Nevermind. I'm happy to be with Hope again.

Hope's participation turns out to be one of many pleasant surprises. Classes are taught by students from Harvard's Masters in Teaching program. They are better teachers than any I've had before, varying their styles, using lots of visual aids and letting us experiment, especially in geometry, with concrete materials. My English teacher opens up a world of ideas that I can relate to. She reads poetry about historical tensions between Irish and Italian immigrants in Boston, and reads it so engagingly I work all summer on my own to memorize every verse in the exact same dialects that she uses. We read stories about the oppression of Jews in Nazi Germany and stories about prejudice against black people in our own country. The vocabulary I'm building through these class discussions – oppression, prejudice, tyranny, shunning, powerlessness, bias, discrimination, injustice and so on – becomes mine. I don't have to work hard to grasp the underlying concepts. These ideas give me new ways of thinking about Priscilla and my role in the family. I am one with the Jews and the black people.

During daily recreation periods, I am the only kid who does not go beyond the roped-in shallow area of the lake. I can't swim. Hope works tirelessly with me every day to teach me how to float, and I finally get it. She gets me to swim underwater and do handstands in the water. But I cannot make myself go out beyond the rope. I get frightened to death when the water is over my head. I can only watch her as she swims out to the raft to play with the others for a while. I stay in shallow water where I feel safe and practice floating face down and face up, so very proud of this accomplishment.

Each day on the bus, I sit with Hope and Annie, an older girl Hope has befriended. Annie is deaf and has very little speech. Hope and I spend the bus ride to and from summer school learning sign language with her and trying to communicate. Hope is much more fluent at it than I am. Here, too, is a lesson in discrimination. Annie is shunned by those who cannot speak in sign language and do not want to understand her circumstances. The other kids go so far as to call her dumb and make fun of her. Hope and I think she is smarter than either of us. I am learning what it means to treat everyone as equals, to have moral convictions and a point of view.

I cannot contain my expanded sense of awareness, of being a participant in a universe of good and evil rather than a lone child going through a solitary hell. The urge to be out in the world rather than confined to my room is so powerful I ask Priscilla every day, just before suppertime, "May I please walk down to the end of the street and meet Dad?"

"I suppose so."

I revel in summer's late afternoon light, the warmth, the green canopy that shades the sidewalk as I walk down to the corner where Marshall Road meets Main Street. I think of things I can tell Dad about school while we walk back home together. When I see him crest the hill from his train station, walk past the rotary and look for a break in the traffic to cross, when I see the straw hat on his head and folded Christian Science Monitor swinging from one hand, that little grin on his face, I am happy. I fling my arms around his waist and get a quick hug in return. I talk to him about swimming, or sign language, or geometry; not prejudice and injustice. But I am happy.

The Terrible Twelves

Priscilla's lips pinch together in a grim, straight line. A parallel furrow plows her brow from one temple to the other. While her mind reels, her jaws clench, imprisoning random spills of thought, chewing the words to pulp. Wrath writes its explosive potential in the intensity of her gaze and velocity of her movements as she slaps the iron around the contours of one of Ed's starched white shirts. A tower of temper has been spiraling up in her all afternoon as she stands at the ironing board, filling the six-foot drying rack with an orderly array of pressed clothes and linens.

Down the street, I'm getting advanced archery lessons from Ruthie. She's so good at it she won prizes this summer. She, in turn, is getting an earful from me about the concepts of prejudice and discrimination. The ideas are new to Ruthie, but she's smart and enjoys talking through some of our grade school history lessons – the Pilgrims and Indians, the Civil War – using this frame of reference. I don't discuss the connections to my home life because I'm too ashamed of being so thoroughly unloved by my own mother.

With just days to go until we start junior high, Ruthie and I also talk about how all the girls will be wearing nylons to school instead of socks, flats instead of shoes with ties or buckles, bras instead of undershirts, and make-up, especially lipstick. I won't be allowed any of that, I know. I raised the issue with my parents when I went downstairs at bedtime a few nights ago. "What makes you think you need a bra?" Priscilla taunted, me with my chest flat as a pancake. "You have nylons we got you for church on Sundays. Why do you need nylons for school? Aren't socks good enough for you?"

"I want to be just like everybody else," I said.

"Well, we don't want you to be just like everybody else," Dad chimed in, grinning. "We want you to be yourself." So I know I'm going to stick out like a sore thumb.

Ruthie tells me she wants to keep wearing socks. "I think they're more comfortable," she says. She speaks from the freedom of knowing her parents will take her thoughts into account and allow her to do what she decides is right for her.

When it's time for me to leave Ruthie's and head home, I saunter up the street with my hands in my pockets. Traces of self-assurance worked their way into my psyche over the course of the summer: the after-glow of finding meaning in new knowledge, learning how to float in the water, mastering sign language, regaining Hope as a friend and feeling prepared for junior high. For just a moment, I forget to dim the light on my face, forget to bring my self-protective, invisible demeanor to the fore as I come in the back door, wipe my feet and traverse the sunlit kitchen floor.

Words come too easily out of my mouth. "Hi, Mum. Ruthie's been giving me some archery lessons today. She's really good at it." That brings me past the rack of pressed clothes, adjacent to the tip of the ironing board.

"I'm not interested in anything you do," Priscilla snarls. I'm almost over the threshold from the kitchen to the hallway. "I HATE YOU!" Priscilla yells at the top of her lungs.

The force of this verbal blast catches me somewhere up around my right shoulder and spins me around. I look at Priscilla, my jaw slack. Priscilla stares back, all movement suspended after her paroxysm, the iron resting on its heel but still in her hand, like a molten fist. Her eyes are a cold, yawning entrance to a loathing machine bent on grinding me to dust. I am stunned that she would use the word hate, which we three kids have been taught is a swear word. At the same time, I am profoundly relieved to have heard her say this at last. An unbidden smile starts to shape itself. Before it becomes visible, I turn away, leap down the hallway and up the stairs.

In my room, I sit on the end of the bed, feet on the foot board. Inside, anatomical cells are buzzing a frenzied tune. I try to analyze what just happened. It energized me. "How come I feel excited? Priscilla finally told me straight out that she hates me and I think it's great? I must be really whacko." Something once knotted up inside like a ball of snippets has loosened, released. Priscilla admitted the underlying theme of our twisted relationship. In three words, she finally spelled out the only vocabulary I need to understand what is happening between us. As I told myself at the age of five, my mother hates me. Having suspected that truth all along, having Priscilla say it feels like a major vindication. For a mother to say "I hate you" to her own child is wrong in the eyes of people everywhere. It can't be undone, taken back or lied about. And Priscilla did it.

I feel powerful, vengeful. Dad wants me to believe that my mother loves me? That all I suffer is in my mind? HA! Wait 'til he hears this! I have something potent to use against Priscilla whenever I choose. If I get desperate sometime, I am going to tell Dad. In fact, maybe I'll tell him tonight! Priscilla lost control, and now it is Priscilla who will have to watch her step. Finally, I'm the one with power in my hands. She's going to have a lot of trouble defending herself, if I ever mention this to Dad. "She said she hates me!" Of course, she'd probably just deny it ever happened.

I decide I'm not going to look her in the eye for a while. Let her wonder what I'm thinking, what I might do with my new-found power.

After a while, sorrow worms its way back inside me. I begin to realize what I just lost. "My mother hates me." The finality of it is devastating. All this time I've been trying to believe that she really does love me, somewhere deep down inside; she just got messed up somewhere along the way with being able to show it. Now I have to let go of that idea.

I don't hate Priscilla. It's unthinkable. I'm in enough trouble all the time for no good reason, all the while trying to be so virtuous. I can't switch gears all of a sudden and allow myself to be a spiteful ball of fury who hates Priscilla; it would ruin my whole image of myself, the me I have to believe in. Imagine if I hated her! If that ever showed in my face or my words, I'd be dead. I've learned to focus positive thoughts on her range of talents and her competence, her deft hands in motion and the things they produce. I hate the Gestapo tactics she uses to make me suffer. I hate her inability to love me, the dynamic I have to live with. I'm deathly afraid of her, to be sure, but I yearn for her in that unrequited way of the child who, having no mother, assumes the one she should have had would have been perfect. "What in the world did I ever do to make Priscilla hate me?" I ask myself for the millionth time.

Suddenly I have a sense of foreboding. Something specific had to have been behind her outburst. I should prepare myself for the other shoe to drop. She must be thinking up some awful new punishment, for her to be that upset with me over nothing. "Oh, God. I'm in for something. I just know it." I hope I can bear up alright.

The other shoe drops on the next ironing day, falling with the faintness of a slipper rather than a kick of the steel-toed boot I feared. "Susan. Get down here," Priscilla calls from the kitchen. Penny is leaning up against the kitchen counter, arms folded, hints of a Cheshire cat smile tugging at the corners of her mouth as she watches me come nervously towards them.

Uh- oh. Penny's in on it, whatever it is. This is not good. She looks like she relishes her role as Priscilla's ally.

"Take those up to your room," Priscilla says, waving the iron at a stack of brochures on the end of the ironing board. "You're to read them until you understand everything. Then bring them down and put them right back here. If you have any questions, ask your sister. She's already read them."

Curious, I take the brochures upstairs and sit on the end of my bed. They have information about breast growth, pubic hair and body odor. They are mostly about female monthly cycles, with a few vague hints about a connection to having babies. Nothing about sex, or about male puberty. I learn that periods, as they're called, are painless, regular and natural. Most girls start having them at about my age. This is the first I've heard of this phenomenon, so I read everything three times to make sure I can remember all of the details.

Modess, the company providing the brochures, assures me that their sanitary pads are comfortable, absorbent and modern. How in the heck do you wear that thing? I finally understand what's in those big boxes that say, "Modess . . . Because," that Priscilla orders over the phone from S.S. Pierce and stashes away in the back of her closet, and why the bathroom wastebaskets sometimes fill up with round things bound up in toilet paper. I wonder if Penny has started yet.

I bring the brochures back downstairs and put them on the end of the ironing board, embarrassed by my new knowledge of such intimate details and determined not to give the two of them the satisfaction of seeing any confusion on my face. I turn to go back upstairs, but Priscilla's tense voice whips out to call me back. "Did you understand what you read?" Penny is still leaning against the counter, pretending to be as nonchalant as an off-duty security guard.

"Yes," I say, and leave it at that.

"Ya, sure," Priscilla says sarcastically. Then more quietly, "Just like you understand half of what you're told."

When the periods come, they are ferocious, excruciating. Every month I am sick all day the first day with severe cramps accompanied by vomiting and bowel movements every half hour. Penny complains to Priscilla once about her own mild cramps, and Priscilla says to her, "You should stay home sometime and see what your sister goes through!"

Priscilla herself has dysmenorrhea. On those monthly mornings, she barely gets a breakfast of cold cereal on the table, then she lays on the couch. When Dad is dressed and we three kids have assembled at the table, Dad goes to the living room and gives his arm to Priscilla. He escorts her, bent over in pain, to the table. She takes a few sips of her tea, her face gray, until Dad says, "Do you need to lie down again, Honey?" She nods, and he escorts her back to the couch. By the time we get home from school, she is up and around and doing her usual household chores.

Not me. When I don't have one end or the other over the toilet bowl, I am on my bed, writhing in pain, moaning aloud. By 3 o'clock in the afternoon, the stomach upset subsides and I am down to coping with the severe cramps. Priscilla, who has some sympathy for this syndrome and listens for signs that I've gone into the next phase, brings me a cup of tea. "Drink this while it's hot," she says, and leaves. The tea acts like a magic potion, loosening the awful cramps, allowing me to drift off into a deep sleep, which lasts through the remains of the afternoon and all night long. I awake cloaked in a blissful sense of euphoria that stays with me throughout the second day, the result of residual morphine my body had been producing to offset the pain.

Junior high. I'm like a foreigner from a third world nation trying to understand the rules of the UN Assembly. With whom do I want to be allied? How do I communicate with a mob of teenagers from the alien culture of normalcy? Should I worry more about dress, smarts, interests or boys? How do I develop a sense of belonging when I don't even belong in my own home? I repeatedly find myself in conversations about matters that are not part of my experience, and I begin to wonder how much discrepancy between school realities and my realities I can tolerate.

Junior high kids study each other every day, evaluating and judging character based on appearance and behavior. Conformity gets nods of approval, but so does blatant non-conformity. Girls with cashmere sweaters and silver charm bracelets like to hang out with boys who keep a pack of cigarettes rolled up in the sleeve of their tee-shirts. Tall, tan, well-dressed boys who probably spend summers sailing on Cape Cod gravitate to gum-popping cheap girls with pierced ears. Behind the goofy laughter and facial expressions of the boy-girl dynamics is the serious message that it's time to get started picking a mate.

Good grooming is everything. Thankfully, I'm allowed to take showers instead of baths now, three nights a week, and I have deodorant. Instead of asking permission to shave my legs, I surreptitiously raid the medicine cabinet to borrow one of Dad's old hand-held razors when I'm in the shower. When I get to school, I take my bobby socks off, put them in my book bag and wear my shoes sockless. I walk the back roads on the way home so I can stop in the shadows somewhere to put my socks back on. I'm a far cry from blending in.

My parents had me read a book by Pat Boone over the summer. It was called Twixt Twelve and Twenty. "Penny read it when she was your age," Dad said when he handed it over. That was the full extent of any discussion with them about the book. It had a lot about teenagers being too immature and confused to understand true love. Frankly, I'm not interested. I haven't got room in my psyche for anything other than dealing with Priscilla, even though I keep envisioning myself as the world's best mother with at least 6 children. Eventually. Right now, the only boys interested in me seem to be weirdos of one kind or another – strutting boys who sense my vulnerability, awkward boys who are nervous wrecks about the whole puberty thing.

Teenage girls fight with their parents over every little thing! It's not just being boy-crazy that creates spats about the limits their parents impose; it's wearing too-tight sweaters and too-short skirts, going on Metrecal diets, talking on the phone, piercing their ears, skipping gym class, staying out late, having messy rooms. They rebel against everything!

Their worst and most frequent arguments are with their mothers. I listen intently to learn how they deal with a mother's anger, but all I get is a sense that those relationships have ups and downs, some more extreme than others. Arguments come and go. The girls yell and pout, slam doors and say what they think, even when it's in direct opposition to what their mothers think. They get grounded all the time, but disagreements don't threaten their position in the family or the love between parent and child.

If I told them the rules I'm living under, they'd think I was lying. When they ask why I don't wear make-up and don't go to the dances, I simply say, "My mother won't let me." That they all understand. It's a common refrain. But I can add nothing further to the girl talk, wouldn't dream of traipsing off to the girl's room for a collective pee break between classes or hanging around with them downtown after school. I'm not allowed to use the phone, have friends over, do things that teens do in groups. I have nothing to say to the entitled majority; they have no idea what my life is like. There is no good reason for anyone to associate with me, much less admire me.

Right off the bat I hate Math and English classes. The two subjects I excelled in over the summer are the ones I dread the most, having little patience for these ancient, bored teachers who stick to their textbooks instead of looking for ways to help students thrive with their subject matter. It is very, very hard to see the blackboard now, even from a front row seat. All these teachers do is talk and write on the board.

Home Economics classes are required for girls. The first year focuses on sewing. What am I going to do? Girls go home and practice threading and running sewing machines with their mothers. Priscilla's sewing machine is off limits to me, so the contraptions at school remain complicated pieces of machinery whose parts I can't even name. Girls in the class work on projects both at school and at home: an apron, a skirt, a blouse. We have to produce something we would actually wear. The school provides the patterns; mothers take their girls to the fabric counters in town to pick out colors and materials together, along with matching threads, buttons and zippers. Mothers show daughters techniques they've learned from years of practice. Priscilla knows this from working with Penny on her seventh grade sewing projects two years ago. Nevertheless, I get cloth and thread flung at me from the doorway of my room, materials that Priscilla has chosen begrudgingly, that I have to beg for at the dinner table several nights in a row so I can do the required work, ineptly, leaning on my scant knowledge from Auntie Belle.

Options to join school teams and clubs multiply – softball, radio, philosophy, drama, tennis. I want to be part of them all. But the inherent parental support that goes along with being involved in these activities is out of the question. How would I pay for a uniform or attend evening events?

Orchestra and singing – those are my fortes. I get to continue playing viola in a school orchestra, sticking to it even when I can tell that my peers think carrying around an instrument case puts me in a lower caste, one reserved for people who are just plain dull to be around. I sing in the girl's glee club and the mixed chorus, and get selected by the music teacher to join an eight-member madrigal chorus. There's only one problem. I can't get permission to go on any of the trips these groups schedule to compete in state and regional competitions for junior high orchestras and choruses. I haven't done anything to deserve that. "Your grades don't warrant going away on school trips" says Priscilla. "You should be home studying to get those grades up."

The girl's gym teacher tries to keep us interested in her class with a wide variety of activities, everything from using the rings and pommel horse, to roller skating and badminton. I'm bad at all of it, one of the unfit, immature, awkward girls who can't get a note from her mother asking the teacher to excuse me from this or that for one trumped up reason or another. Even more embarrassing is putting on an undershirt in front of everyone after taking the mandatory shower at the end of class.

The fates intervene briefly on my behalf. A piece of grit gets stuck under the skin of my right hand and becomes infected. Priscilla has me soaking it every night in very hot water. She makes a bandage smeared with a stick of brown stuff that she melts with a match. The infection grows from a little bump, to the size of a dime, then a quarter, and on and on until it covers my palm. By the end of each school day it is heavy with pus. Priscilla makes Dad take a look at it one night, gives him a visual aid to help him decide if this is reason enough to go to a doctor. "Yikes!" he says. "How do you stand the water being that hot?"

"I'm just used to it," I say.

They stick with the home remedy. The bandage covers my whole hand. I cannot participate in gym for a couple of months. Yippee. "It's all the bad in you coming out," Priscilla says. Finally, finally, it starts to dry up.

The assumption that each student will go on to get a college education is rampant – in my conversations with classmates, in teacher's comments, in the courses everyone is taking. At home, Priscilla says, "What's wrong with being a secretary? Not good enough for you, Your Highness? You're just looking down your nose at secretaries." She and Dad think all this is easy, a given that involves no decision-making. I should be doing what my sister did: getting ready to enter the high school business education track, with classes in Latin, bookkeeping, shorthand and typing.

Priscilla tells Penny to loan me her freshman Gregg shorthand books and tell me to try it out. "Just start at the beginning and follow the instructions," Penny says, dumping the books on my bureau. "You might like it." But I hate it. I have no talent for duplicating doodles and squiggles. Boring, boring, boring. I haven't a shred of interest in the things secretaries learn and do. Pick your battles as they say. This is the most important one to me.

I hand the books back to Penny. "I don't like it. I can't do it."

For once I don't want to follow in Penny's footsteps. She has no mind of her own, she's become so geared to pleasing her parents over the years. Besides, being a secretary is so old-fashioned. I don't know anyone in my class who is excited by that idea. All my friends and 85% of the student body are signing up for the college-bound course of study. I want to be in the majority, part of the norm. I've had enough of being different.

Visions of myself as an adult start to intrude into the present, ideas about someday needing to work until I am married with children. What do I want to do for work?

"You're not going to stay here and expect us to keep paying for a roof over your head," Priscilla says at the dinner table. "What are you going to do with yourself?"

"I want to be an actress," I reply.

"You don't need a college education to be an actress," Priscilla snorts.

The pressure is fierce at school to pre-register for one of the particular tracks of courses the high school offers: college prep, secretarial, industrial arts/home economics. The only other freshman option is labeled "general," the one for people who need another year to decide. My heart and soul know with a clarity beyond words that I need to go to college, but that addled brain of mine keeps coming up empty when I try to identify a career for me.

Meanwhile at home, Priscilla challenges me time after time. "Just give us one good reason why your father should spend a fortune putting you through college when you've done nothing to show us that you'll put any effort into your school work. Your grades certainly don't look like someone who's college material."

Then one night, in the midst of another going-nowhere clash of wills about this at the dinner table, she blurts out the answer as if she, too, has been agonizing over this question. "Why don't you be a teacher?" she says. "You like little kids." I breathe out a huge gust of relief. I am going to college. I will have a career. I will not be forced to take the secretarial courses. Dad must have decided to support the idea, and told Priscilla.

"OK," I say, smiling. Battle won. If I will be a teacher, I can go to college, so I will be a teacher. Even though I'm an amorphous creature trying to remain invisible while I manage Priscilla's threats to my well-being, I am a college-bound future teacher.

The invisible child walks downtown to the junior high every day with a bunch of neighborhood kids, picking up other friends on the corners of intersecting streets. Somewhere out there, some people don't like what they see. I arrive home from school one day to find Priscilla crying at her sewing machine. "Get in here," she says when I pass by. "Read that," Priscilla says, indicating a letter that lays open on the end of the sewing machine table. Except for the light on the sewing machine, the room is dark, so I go over to the windows to read the letter, dropping my books on a chair as I go.

"Dear Mrs. Dalziel," it begins, the handwriting beautiful, precise. "We hate you. Why don't you buy Susan some new clothes? Her red hat, green overcoat and black galoshes look terrible." My heart sinks to the floor. The letter goes on for a full two pages about what a good person I am and what an awful mother Priscilla is. I try to memorize the whole thing but the stress is too great.

"Who wrote that?" Priscilla asks, her voice clogged from crying. "You tell me who wrote that, and don't say 'I don't know' because I bet you put them up to it. Who wrote that?"

"I don't know," is all I can say, shaking my head. "I have no idea."

"Well you'd better figure it out before your father gets home. Go to your room. I can't stand the sight of you."

I cannot believe someone would put me in such jeopardy. Whoever wrote that letter has to know how bad things are for me already. Now it is going to get worse in ways I can't even imagine.

The truth is, I hate having to wear Penny's old dark green overcoat with the cloth belt. It's ugly and way too big for me. The bright red hat showed up under the Christmas tree; I've been trying to weasel out of wearing it ever since. It's all fuzzy on top and has cloth that comes down over my ears and ties at the throat. An out-dated, ridiculous Vermont Country Store hat. It clashes with the coat – anyone can see that. The galoshes – black buckle galoshes for goodness sake, when everyone else wears real boots and tucks their shoes in their book bags. It's bad. I've been dressed like that all winter.

I can barely eat dinner. When Dad calls me downstairs after supper I am trembling with fear. "We want to know who wrote that letter," he says sharply.

"I don't know, Dad. I have been thinking and thinking about it and I can't think of anyone who would do that."

"Your mother looked all over for a hat like that for you for Christmas," he says, Priscilla's ardent defender. "She wanted something to keep your ears warm so you wouldn't catch cold. It's not right that you keep complaining about it." Pause. Silence. "This sounds like something one of your friends would say." His voice is low, hard, angry.

"Dad, I don't think any of my friends would do this."

"Well it's up to you to find out who did. Until you find out who did it, you're not to leave for school until everyone else is gone. You can walk by yourself to school. And you're to come home immediately after school, by yourself. Do you understand?"

Every night that week he comes to my room after dinner and asks me who wrote the letter. Every night I name more people that I have asked about it, which has been a painful, embarrassing thing to do but I have done it. "I can't think of anyone else to ask," I tell him at the end of the first week.

"Then you can keep walking to school by yourself again next week," he says. "Until you tell us who wrote that letter, you are going to walk to school by yourself." Week after week this scene with Dad repeats.

The moment I read the letter I suspected it did not come from any of my classmates. Teenagers are so preoccupied with themselves and their own parental battles it wouldn't occur to them to write a letter like that. The letter was too well worded and the penmanship was too lovely for someone of my age. I think it was Mrs. Ball and Mrs. Davis, colluding again on my behalf. But that is not a thought I can say out loud, so I walk to school alone for the remainder of the winter. In my green coat, red hat and black galoshes.

The Asian flu spreads through the general population like wildfire. So many kids are out of school the administrators are deciding day by day whether to close or not. Somewhere between first and second period classes on a Monday morning, the flu finds me.

The school nurse sticks a thermometer under my tongue, making me even more nauseous. "Call her mother," the nurse sings out to the school secretary in the adjacent office. I lurch for the toilet.

"Susan's throwing up, her temperature is sub-normal and she's white as a sheet," the secretary says to Priscilla. "She's probably got this awful flu that's going around. We're dismissing her."

"She can walk home," Priscilla says. "I have no way to get her."

"She's very sick!" the secretary responds, shocked at Priscilla's disregard for my illness. "Can someone else come and get her?"

"Tell her to walk," Priscilla says testily. "I've got a very sick mother here to care for! I don't drive and I'm not going to impose on anyone to cater to her. She can walk home."

It has been snowing so often this winter the sidewalks are a moonscape of pitted boot tracks with mountains of snow on both sides. The air has been arctic for days; the wind is biting. I don't know how I'm going to make it home, upset stomach and all. Thinking about the hen-clucks of sympathy and concern that come from school nurses and secretaries,

I want another mother. I want to be taken care of. I am afraid I might faint and fall so deep down in the snow no one will be able to see me.

By the time I reach Marshall Road, a mile away, I am stumbling, weaving, wooing my stomach like a lover. "Just a few more steps. We can do it. Hold on now." I wobble up the stairs to the back porch, make it through boot and coat removal in the back entryway, walk with my book bag through the kitchen to the dining room, heading for the stairway with a shaky, "Hi," in the direction of Grammie's room. Priscilla is seated in there, talking idly to her mother, who lays under her bedcovers somewhere back in the shadows.

Without looking up from her needlepoint or turning around, Priscilla says, "There are two aspirin on the corner of the dining table there. Bring them upstairs with you and take them."

My hand fumbles at the small white tablets sitting stark against a dark tablecloth. The last ounces of true grit have ebbed away. I am spent. The hell with the aspirin. It's all I can do to make it upstairs to vomit.

For the rest of the day, I vomit every twenty minutes. At noon Priscilla calls up the stairs, "Your Highness. Will you be coming down for lunch?"

"No."

The constant retching continues through the night. The next day, I watch the hands on my clock record some progress – the attacks are now an hour or two apart. By the third day, I feel despair. The longest my stomach has been quiet is four hours; my abdominal muscles are so sore I have trouble falling asleep in between trips to the toilet.

Each morning Dad comes to my door and asks, "Can you get up and go to school today?"

"No."

The third day passes. In the middle of the night I am once again crouched in the bathroom, hugging the porcelain base of the toilet, a pile of worthless flesh and bones on the cold linoleum floor. I can only imagine

Priscilla's wrath at having her sleep disturbed once again, at having to listen to my racket coming through the wall behind her pillow.

I hear the bed behind the wall creak, hear feet hit the floor, hear steps coming. I don't care. I don't care what either one of them has to say about my lack of concern for other family members who need their sleep, sleep I have probably interrupted over and over again for three nights in a row. I'm too sick to put energy into being inaudible. My stomach will not stop its relentless heaving.

Dad opens the door. He sits on the side of the tub and rubs my back in a gentle, circular motion. The gesture tells me he got up to be with a sick child, not to scold me. That surprises me. For the first time in three days, someone in the family has come to offer me comfort. I retch again. Dad is too concerned to feed me Christian Science dogma. "There's nothing left inside of you to make you sick," he explains, his voice soothing, sure. "You're all done with this. It's all gone. You've gotten rid of everything that was in your stomach. You need to go back to bed now and get some sleep."

I believe him – suddenly, utterly. He's my Dad. He got up with me in the middle of the night and tried to comfort me. He knows these things. He must be right. Dad wets a washcloth at the sink and hands it to me so I can wipe the damp coolness over my face. I go back to bed and will my stomach to be calm, wanting to please my father, who just got out of bed to treat me like a daughter. I sleep through the rest of the night and much of the fourth day.

Not since Monday noon has Priscilla called up the stairs to see if I want lunch or anything else. She has not come to my room to assess how I am doing, to offer ginger ale, to take my temperature. She has skipped the bedtime ritual of checking my curtains and closing the door. Neither Penny nor Stephen has stopped by to ask how I am. I haven't seen or spoken to anyone in the household except for Dad, when he asks me about going to school in the mornings, and when he got up with me in the night.

On Friday morning, Dad comes to the door and asks hopefully, "Do you think you're ready to go back to school today?"

Susan D. Anderson

Knowing it will disappoint him, I say, "No." I feel like I could just go on and on like this, staying in bed, not eating, getting weaker and weaker until I die.

Around mid-afternoon, though, Priscilla calls up the stairs. "Susan. You get yourself out of bed, get dressed, and get down here! You make your bed before you come down here, too." My slow-moving body parts do not want to cooperate with any of those commands, but I have no choice. I finally make it down to the arch to the living room, prop myself there while I try to figure out the next step. Priscilla comes around from the kitchen with a tall glass of thick, pale yellow frothy liquid that has just come out of the blender.

"Take this." She shoves it into my hand. "Drink it slowly. Walk around the edge of the living room while you're drinking it. Just sip it and keep walking. You have to get something into you. I'm not going to wait on you hand and foot." She wipes her hands against her apron as if fearing contamination from a leper and walks away.

I drag myself around and around the perimeter of the living room, sipping the strange concoction for long minutes. All alone. It tastes something like a milk shake, but it is not sweet. Maybe an eggnog? Whatever it is, it must be meant to bring someone back from the brink of dehydration and starvation because that's what it does. I finally feel like I might live through this.

Back in my room, I lie on top of the covers and review the events of the week. I became aware on Tuesday that Priscilla was ignoring my existence; by Wednesday the absence of even a call up the stairs was as plain as the nose on my face. And here it is Friday. I drift off to sleep again.

I get called for supper. It's the first meal I've had since breakfast on Monday. "It's good to see you up and dressed," Dad says.

"Ya. About time Her Highness decided to come to the table," Priscilla says. "Have you gotten enough attention now for being sick?"

I snap back at Priscilla, "You haven't come upstairs or even asked if I wanted anything once since Monday lunch time, when I had just come home and was sick every few minutes. That was the only time you called upstairs."

Priscilla's jaw drops at the audacity of my retort. She shoots me a look of withering disbelief, but I stare right back at her without flinching. "Wha!" Her response is a splutter. "Wha! I did so!"

But for once in his life, Dad cuts her off. "That's enough!" he says sharply. Priscilla looks down at her plate, purses her lips and shuts up.

Trial Separations

At the breakfast table, there's a big clue that something's afoot. Dad's not dressed for work. Here it is the middle of the week and he has on a sports shirt and pants he usually wears on weekends. Across the table, Priscilla's eyes are red-rimmed, her face exhausted. She rubs a hand across it while Dad looks at his plate and says, "Your grandmother died last night."

We three kids are instantly upset, murmuring, "Oh no!" and "I'm sorry" to Priscilla. Our parents have been going to the hospital every night for weeks to see Grammie, but we three kids thought she'd be coming home again. She always came home.

"When is the funeral," Penny asks.

"In a couple of days," Dad says.

"Can we go?" I ask. I want to see Grammie again.

"Funerals aren't for children," Priscilla says. "You three kids are to go to school, keep your thoughts to yourselves. There's no need to be blabbing about this."

"Just behave yourselves," Dad adds. "Mind your own affairs. It's nobody's business but our own."

In the weeks that immediately follow, Priscilla is so tired and sad that she hasn't got the energy to get after me. She still gives me those withering looks, still speaks to me only when necessary, harshly. But her eyes are downcast; she is quiet, preoccupied with memories of her Mummer.

Susan D. Anderson

A storage company from Boston unloads a truck full of boxes and furniture in our cellar. Auntie Belle and Uncle Bud's family come for a day of dividing up everything. The grownups traipse down cellar to make decisions about wing back chairs, footstools, lamps and tables. Then one by one Dad and Uncle Bud bring boxes up from the cellar. The women open each one up on the dining table, spread out the contents and decide who will get what. There's silverware, dishes, fancy platters and bowls, kitchen gadgets, linens, embroidery. Every once in a while they call Lynn and Penny and me into the dining room and hand out sun hats, hankies, gloves and scarfs. There's plenty to go around. When Grammie saw something she liked, she bought one in every color. It's all very old fashioned, though.

Things settle down again. Sort of. I overhear a couple of phone calls that make Dad so angry he bellows into the phone. "Listen. There is no reason for this. My wife has had enough of this run around. You get this settled NOW. If you can't resolve this by the end of the week, we're getting another lawyer. This should all have been taken care of months ago." Slam goes the phone back into its cradle. So unlike Dad.

Then the biggest surprise of all. "Susan. Put your jacket on and come outside," Dad calls up quietly from the bottom of the stairs one Saturday. He and Priscilla have been busy every weekend lately doing yard work, so I suppose I'll be asked to help clean up some piles of brush or something. I come down through the cellar and out the door to the back yard. There on the blacktop is a big, red brand new bike.

"Grammie left you a few dollars and said she wanted you to get a bicycle with that money," Dad tells me. "She left a little something for Penny and Stephen, too." I can't believe my eyes and ears.

"This bike is for me?" This means Grammie wanted to do something very special for me, and she was willing to go against Priscilla's wishes to do it. That bowls me over.

Typically, Priscilla has to get a few nasty comments off her chest. "Don't think I don't know you've been deliberately disobeying me. You've been riding Ruthie's bike behind my back, haven't you? You don't deserve this any more than you deserve anything else."

But her words lack punch, what with that gold emblem that says "Collegiate" beaming at me from the frame of my very own beautiful red bicycle. "Can I go ride it?" I ask, afraid it's going to be taken away if I so much as blink.

"You can ride it over in the schoolyard for now," says Dad. "You'll need to take it down to the police station to get a license plate before you can ride it on the streets." They're going to let me ride it on the streets? Wow. That will be a huge change.

I don't ask permission; I start telling Priscilla, truthfully, where I am going on my bike after school. I am a free child now, out of her sight as I ride and ride and ride my bike. I walk it proudly downtown to get my license plate at the police station, go to the gas station to check the air in the tires at least twice a week, ride to the tennis courts, finding other excuses to be out of the house and on my bike every day after school, still stunned by my good fortune. Not once does Priscilla threaten to take it away.

I start haunting the library, sitting by the duck pond reading a book with the bike on the ground beside me. Priscilla only allows me to take out three books at a time, so I choose the fattest ones with the smallest print when I go home: Last of the Mohicans, Les Miserables, Ivanhoe, Lorna Doone. The rule is that I must leave them on top of the radiator in the front hallway for Priscilla to check before she allows me to take them up to my room to read. She gets around to that when she pleases, and the waiting is agony.

Meanwhile, Dad and Priscilla put their energy into creating new spaces and new ways of living their life on Marshall Road. They start by changing Grammie's room into a cozy den. Dad gets a multi-drawer desk with a glass top; Priscilla organizes a sewing nook by the side windows and lines up new sewing projects. They sit there on Sunday afternoons and after dinner in the evenings: reading, paying bills, writing letters, talking and listening to music until their favorite TV shows come on. Dad goes in there after breakfast every day, closes the door to block out the family's bustle and reads his daily Christian Science passages in peace and quiet before he leaves for work. He used to have to do his morning readings in the living room.

Penny starts doing her homework at the dining table after dinner, spreading it out all around her, right outside the den so she can ask Priscilla questions about shorthand and talk to Dad about bookkeeping. Stephen plays with his toys in the living room until Penny, Dad and Priscilla are ready to gather there to watch TV. They have a color TV now, and a lot of programs that make them laugh.

Now that Priscilla is alone during the day and can take a little time to relax, she brings her lunch into the living room and stays there for a while, reading magazines and watching Queen for a Day before she goes back to her household chores. As the baseball season gets underway, Dad teaches her how to keep a score card so she can watch the Boston Braves day games. For him she spends entire afternoons glued to the couch, watching televised games like a hawk, keeping meticulous play by-play records on yellow legal paper so she can tell him all about the players stats when he gets home. I love to hear the game on when I come home, knowing that means I have a clear path to my room and no worries that Priscilla will come after me there.

I am lying in bed listening to Dad brush his teeth, thinking about what to wear to school. Suddenly the sense that something is wrong jolts me upright. The aural cues I am so used to in the mornings are off kilter. Priscilla has not gotten up yet, although I can hear Dad already beginning to shave. She is usually sliding her closet door open, getting her robe and slippers on and heading downstairs to start breakfast by the time he's brushing his teeth. An anxious feeling starts burbling around my stomach as I sit on the edge of my bed, straining my ears, willing Priscilla's morning routine to begin, trying to think up logical reasons why it's not.

Finally I hear faint noises, sounds that freeze me in fear. Priscilla is trying to knock on the wall behind her bed to get Dad's attention. I'm sure that's what it is. The tapping is weak, three hesitant raps that don't cut through the drone of his razor. I start shaking, wondering if I imagined the sound. I can hear Penny and Stephen getting dressed for school in their rooms. Don't they realize that something is wrong? Can somebody please do something?

Panic rises. Should I go get Dad, knock on the bathroom door? Come on, Dad! Turn off your razor! Sensing Priscilla's distress and not knowing what to do about it, my trembling worsens as another minute passes. Again I hear three raps, a little stronger this time, and then Priscilla's desperate, thread-thin voice crying, "Eddie!" Oh, God! What's wrong? Did he hear?

Unsure whether he heard something or not, Dad shuts off his razor and listens, hearing nothing. Still puzzled, he comes out of the bathroom and peeks into their room. Priscilla moans. Their voices murmur low as they try to keep this between them, this crisis. Priscilla is very, very sick. Sick enough to whimper. Sick enough to say to Dad in near-incoherent feverishness, "I need a doctor! You have to get me a doctor! Get him to come here right now! I've got to have a doctor, got to have a doctor."

Dad's response is calm, reassuring. He tells her over and over, "It's OK, Honey. Just stay there and rest. I'll take care of everything, Shhh, shhh. It's OK."

He throws on his casual clothes and goes downstairs, calling the doctor first, then his boss. He races us through a breakfast of cold cereal and sends us off to school with a brief explanation. "Your mother's not feeling well so I am going to stay home with her today." If he is having flashbacks of watching his father take charge of their household when he and Ralph were roughly the same ages that Penny and I are, he's not showing it.

The doctor comes and goes, writing prescriptions that Dad rushes to pick up at the drug store as soon as Penny gets home from school and can take his place at Priscilla's bedside. Late in the day, Dad calls his boss again. "My wife is extremely sick. I'm going to be staying home with her all week."

When I overhear this conversation, I start crying. I try to think up diseases that fit what little I know, which is that Priscilla is too sick to get out of bed. Cancer? Tuberculosis? Pneumonia? The door to her bedroom is closed. She doesn't make a sound, not a cough or a whimper. Mentally I berate the family for being unwilling to talk openly about such things, leaving me no room to ask. She might die! I hate myself when I'm suddenly struck by the thought that I wish she *would* die and leave Dad to run the family. He'd be good at it.

We limp through the week on dinners of hot dogs and grilled cheese sandwiches. Upstairs, Priscilla is silent. Dad returns to work the next week and has Penny stay home from school to care for Priscilla, who remains in bed fighting powerful and pervasive symptoms of physical collapse. A severe case of jaundice, an arhythmic heartbeat, utter weakness, high fever: these are the only details I can glean from eavesdropping.

"Can I stay home and help next week, Dad?" I ask, knowing Priscilla would absolutely hate to see my face but wanting to play a role. "I want to help. I could learn how to cook or do the laundry." But we all know this won't work. The family needs helpers who could do some housework but who would also be welcomed by Priscilla as caregivers when she needs assistance. Dad stays home again.

For several more weeks we live on baloney and infrequent laundry, doing our best to keep the house tidy and clean. Dad and Penny swap off the caregiver role and do the grocery shopping and the cooking together. The doctor comes a couple of times each week to treat Priscilla's complete loss of vitality.

The first major sign of progress is when Priscilla manages to come downstairs for a while each day to lie on the couch and watch TV. At that point she can get through the mornings on her own. Dad goes back to work. Penny comes home from school at lunchtime and Priscilla instructs her in how to make dinner, what to put on the grocery list, what to get from the Cushman's bakery truck that comes twice a week and from S.S. Pierce when they call for her monthly order. By the time I get home from school, she's back in bed.

A couple of weeks later, Priscilla gets dressed in the mornings before she goes down to the couch for the day, but that is the extent of her activity. She reluctantly gives in to Dad's request to include me in the process of helping out after school. "Penny needs a chance to catch up on her homework assignments," he says, "and Susan's been asking to help." Priscilla is so helpless she manages a temporary truce, allows me to set up the ironing board by the couch with my back to the TV. She instructs me in the proper sequence of steps for ironing blouses, Dad's boxer shorts, Stephen's and Dad's pants and shirts, and everything else piled sky high in the ironing basket.

She's dressed, but unable to sit up on the couch so she's propped up against a corner with pillows. Her voice sounds achingly weak; her body looks as if someone vacuumed out the bones. But we stay neutral. Priscilla never loses her temper or becomes impatient with my efforts. I don't try to make more of it than it is – a simple case of doing what needs to be done, not a sign of better things to come. The only thing at stake is that I can assume responsibility for doing the family's ironing for as long as the family needs me to do it.

"You seem happier," my Sunday School teacher says. "Your face looks more relaxed lately. I've seen you smile more." Her comments catch me by surprise. Perhaps it's true. The family dynamic shifted dramatically out of necessity these past three months, and I have benefited from that.

As Priscilla slowly lengthens short stints of light housekeeping into being up and around all day, I find myself hoping that her illness was therapeutic on many levels. I'm looking for a transformed mother who has had time to think about how awful she has made my life, and who has decided she is going to do better by me from here on. Prostate with exhaustion, her hands uncharacteristically empty and idle for weeks, perhaps Priscilla spent time trying to decipher the reasons behind her behavior with me. She is forty-three years old and has never before been out from under her mother's yoke of expectations and standards, never lived outside the role of the perfect daughter who could do no wrong. Even as an adult she has never ventured beyond that framework of duty and responsibility to her mother. Now that she is free to be her own woman, will she change? What will she be like?

My bionic ears can now reach through walls and into corners of the house far distant from my upstairs bedroom. Worlds of meaning emerge from a footfall, a fry pan rattled or a faucet turned on. Making sense of the sounds I hear has become second nature, even more important than trying to listen in on conversations that might give me clues about these people and their family life.

Saturday morning sounds are a cinch, because the same ritual unfolds week after week. After breakfast cleanup, animated conversation among Priscilla, Dad, Penny and Stephen moves from the kitchen into the elbow of the downstairs hallway, where the coat closet is. Hangers clang as people whip their jackets off the rack; air swishes as arms thread through silky linings. Voices quiet. Priscilla moves to the open part of the hallway to intone, "Susan. Get your jacket on."

I usually have a foot on my threshold by then. Everyone else is ready, hands reaching for the doorknob to the cellar door, pulling it open, tromping down the wooden stairs, around the bikes that lean against load-bearing poles, past the little workshop room on the right and the laundry room on the left, then out the cellar door, down the walk and around to the garage. Racing behind them from upstairs, I zip up and try to catch up, knowing that if any conversation is going to come my way it is likely to be, "Get a move on, Susan! Pick up your feet! We haven't got all day."

One Saturday morning, there is no, "Susan. Get your coat on." I hear them descending the cellar stairs and wait in the doorway of my room, grinning at their folly, fully expecting to hear one of them come back when they realize they have forgotten me. No one does. The heavy latch of the outside cellar door clicks as it drops into place; the garage door rattles open, car doors bang, the motor starts and revs. I move to my side window to watch in disbelief as the green Pontiac sedan rises to the top of the driveway and turns left on its way to town.

I can't see if they are all in the car but my ears have already told me without a doubt that all four of them have left. Unwilling to believe it, I wait in absolute stillness for some whisper of a sound to give away the presence of someone left behind. Maybe it is a trick to see if they can catch me sneaking about the house when I am supposed to stay in my room. I sit on the edge of my bed. Hold my breath. Listen to the ticking of the mantle clock, the whir of the refrigerator, the intervals of insane cuckoo clock calls from the dining room. I wait for my ears to bring me the information I need, but I hear nothing.

After an hour or so, I get up the courage to go down the hallway and use the bathroom. Otherwise I stay stock still, proving to the ghosts that I am a good girl. The only reason for leaving me behind has to be that I am being punished for something awful that Priscilla isn't going to tell me about until she is damn good and ready.

Hours later they come back - doors banging, voices joshing, shopping bags rustling. Will they check to see if I am alive? How will they know I am still here? I could have run away while they were gone! Wanting them to fear the worst, I make not a sound as they quickly put away the groceries and sundries so they can have lunch. "Susan," Priscilla intones from the bottom of the stairs. I hold back for a few heartbeats, wishing they would at least worry about me a little. Why didn't I take the chance to run away?

At the dining table, I wait for someone to say something to me about why I was left behind. They continue to chat amongst themselves. No eye contact with me, no comments directed towards me, no mention of the crime that led to my punishment. My thoughts turn ugly. Surely Dad will have a word with me? How could he have just gone along with this idea of Priscilla's – not just the part about leaving me, but the part about not even telling me I was going to be left? How does he argue that one with himself? How does it fit into his all-good world?

Over the passing of baloney and bread, I come to see how foolish my expectations have been to think anyone will say anything. On the brink of tears, I realize I'm just a boarder in this establishment. I have a room and I eat my meals at the dining table with the owners. Like some kind of Cinderella, I have to earn my keep by doing household chores. I don't deserve to be given the time of day, as far as Priscilla is concerned. The family foursome has colluded in silence for so long now about so many things where I am concerned that this latest gambit will go as unremarked as all the rest. There is, after all, nothing strange to these people about acting as if I don't exist.

Just like that, we have a new, unspoken Saturday morning ritual. I am to be left at home alone – a practice I slowly begin to relish. There are so many forms of release in those hours of solitude. Unconfined, I use my freedom to explore everything in the house: the attic, the drawers and pigeon holes of the secretary in the living room, the workshop down cellar, everyone's bureau drawers, the junk drawer in the kitchen.

I find my grandfather's Scottish kilt and a set of bagpipes up in the attic, all of it laid reverently across one of the old army surplus cots that are stored in a room up there. If only I dared to pick up the bagpipe! I would love to try to play it, but it is arranged on the bed with such precision I don't dare touch it.

In the back of one of my mother's bureau drawers, behind the folded nylon briefs that are so wide I think I could fit my whole body inside one leg, I find a box of elegant pink and gray stationary that Aunt Lorraine gave me for Christmas. When Priscilla saw me open it she said, "That's too good for the likes of you. You give that to me. When you've done something to earn it, we'll see about it."

Emboldened by that discovery, I go downstairs one night and say, "I want to write a letter to Aunt Lorraine, but I can't find that nice stationary she gave me. Do you know where it is?"

"I'll have to look," Priscilla says. But she does give it back.

In the junk drawer in the kitchen, hidden in back of hammers and light bulbs, is a box of caramel flavored Ayds candy, which, the box says, is an appetite suppressant. I'm not surprised that Priscilla is unhappy about her weight, but coming upon this proof that such a perfect being has a sense of imperfection is refreshing.

I look high and low for pictures of me, and not just because my school picture isn't displayed on top of the piano with Penny's and Stephen's. I have copies of my school pictures. But I do not have pictures of me before I entered school, of when I was a baby, of when a mother and father might have held me like a baby, of when an older sister and I might have played together. Dad always has his latest camera equipment with him wherever we go. Uncle Ralph is a professional photographer who has chronicled every family get-together. I come across tons of pictures that the two of them have taken, so where are the pictures of we three kids in general and me in particular? If I was ever in some family photographs, they have either been buried or tossed out with the trash. I find my birth certificate, and that is a mixed blessing. No longer can I fantasize that I am really Aunt Lorraine's illegitimate child, given to Ed and Priscilla to raise.

I make no noise on my archeological excursions through the household civilization. No TV shows, no music on the stereo. Noise would prevent me from hearing an unexpected return, or a sentry in hiding just waiting pounce. I would love to call Aunt Lorraine, but I know the long distance charge would show up on the phone bill.

I am free to eat on Saturday mornings. As long as I can figure out how to leave every cracker container, cheese package, and olive jar looking exactly the way I found it. As long as I leave no crumbs. I go back to my room an hour or so before the family is due back, a small stack of Waverly Wafers stuck together with sweet maple butter from the Vermont Country Store on a napkin at my side. I pull my chair up to the front window, put my feet on the radiator. In keeping with my status in the family, I was given "50 ways to play solitaire" for Christmas, which came with a mini deck of cards and a slotted lap board for laying out the cards. With the solitaire game board propped on my knees, playing clock solitaire, I eat my Waverly Wafers and wait for the car to return.

One other freedom of movement occurs on those days. The minute Priscilla is gone, my bowels move. The more weeks go by with no Priscilla on Saturday mornings, the more productive my bowels become on Saturday mornings. Otherwise, my bowels have somehow adapted to the extreme stress of living with Priscilla by pretending not to exist.

There are a couple of other signs of the effects Priscilla's tyranny is having on me. I discover a bulging scrapbook down cellar in the laundry room. It is full of greeting cards my mother and father have exchanged over the years on all of the conventional occasions. Signed, "Devotedly yours, Pris," and "All my love, Ed," these must mean a great deal to Priscilla to be saved like this. They have extremely romantic sentiments and look like they were among the most expensive items in the card aisles. I've come to think of my parent's marriage as a business arrangement more than any kind of romance, but the cards tell a different story. They make me believe that the two people I've been sure couldn't possibly love each other in a romantic sense truly do. I start taking little bits of pretty things off of the cards and hoarding them in my room – the little satin bows, the lace, the clever little tin mirrors and cloth flowers that are attached. On Saturday mornings, without realizing the cumulative effects of my petty thievery, I slowly mutilate this beautiful archive of my parents' love.

One Saturday I decide to scratch and scratch under my eye until I create a bleeding abrasion there. Self-mutilation this time. I get my colored pencils and color all around the abrasion with yellows, greens, and blues. It is quite a realistic bruise, I think.

Well, that gets a rise out of Priscilla. "What happened to your eye?" she says, staring at it across the dining table when I sit down for lunch.

"I dropped the phone in your room when I went to answer it," I say. "Banged my face on the radiator." That ought to keep her worried.

"Who was it?" she says.

"Wrong number."

"There's no need for you to answer the phone. Just let it ring."

The next Saturday, with the eye still scabbed where I'd scratched and scratched to make it bleed, I get the colored pencils out and bruise the other eye the same way. No one says a word when I go down for lunch.

❀ ❀ ❀

Dad seems to be looking for new things to do. Do-it-yourself books and magazines start to pile up by his chair; he wants a hobby. Finally, he gets himself a workbench and fancy jigsaw for carpentry projects, sets it up down cellar, and fills the house every weekend with the racket of his sawing and hammering.

One Saturday afternoon, he calls me down from my room. Sitting in the middle of the kitchen floor is a small cabinet, his first finished product. "I made you a nightstand," he says with a grin.

"Wow!" I smile at him, and walk all around it, tickled by his surprise. It has a door on the bottom with two shelves inside, and a second level with an open cubby area topped by a half-shelf. He has painted it light yellow, a color that will work just fine with the red plaid wallpaper and rose colored bedspread. Besides, the knowledge that his first project is something for me infuses this gift with special meaning and value.

Dad talks with great animation to Uncle Bud and Uncle Ralph about his new saw when the next holiday rolls around and all the relatives are gathered at our house for the big meal. "Come upstairs and see the nightstand I made for Susan!" he says. He's forgotten: they haven't been upstairs since we first moved in, when the train set was in the middle of the floor of the once spacious master bedroom. He gets to my bedroom doorway, a small army of uncles and cousins behind him, hesitates a little, then goes in. The visitors keep glancing at my sporty wallpaper as they listen to him talk about making the nightstand. But the next time friends and relatives are visiting they do not get an invitation to come up to my room. He takes them down cellar to see his workbench instead.

Dad has so much vacation time now that he saves an occasional day to do special things with Priscilla. When I see him in his sports shirt at the breakfast table, I know he is taking a day off; he and Priscilla will be doing household projects or enjoying a day trip by themselves.

On one of these excursions, they buy 30 acres of woodland on a hilltop outside of Brattleboro, Vermont. Having spotted the ad for this property in the Boston Globe, suddenly my father is a dreamer. He envisions clearing the land, building a house, getting his CPA and moving to Vermont, where he will have his own tax consultant business and become a Christian Science Practitioner on the side. The image fits nicely with his favorite hymn, "How beautiful upon the mountain are the feet of those who bring peace."

I should have known he'd fallen in love with Vermont. For the past year we've been visiting his Aunt Jessie and Uncle Willy who have come up from New York City to retire in Brattleboro. They're in the process of building their own house up there. After the first visit, Dad was so gung ho on Vermont we kept going back to spend long weekends with them. We three kids slept on mattresses on the bare floors upstairs, while the grownups slept in finished rooms downstairs.

Penny and I had some sister time those weekends, sitting cross-legged on our shared mattress during a couple of rainy days. We looked through back issues of Seventeen magazine. She showed me an article about taking an old nylon stocking and wrapping a pony tail around it at night to turn it into a springy long curl. I tried it on my pony tail that night and it worked so well I kept that hairdo all through junior high.

Priscilla packed enough food for everyone on these visits, and took responsibility for preparing all the meals. Dad bought paint-by-number sets and puzzle books to keep we three kids quiet and out of the way, while all day long Priscilla and Dad helped Aunt Jessie and Uncle Willie grout bathroom tiles, sand countertops, put up drywall, paint cabinets and lay down flooring.

However, it turned out the price of being good guests was higher for Priscilla and Ed than just making themselves useful. Aunt Jessie called my parents into her living room for a confrontation just before we left that last time. "This is no way for a mother to treat a child, Pete," Jessie said angrily, Willie standing stone-faced at her side. "You have no cause to get after Susan for every little thing all day long the way you do. Why on earth are you making her out to be some kind of criminal? Not once have I heard you speak to her kindly. There is no good reason for it. Ed, for goodness sake speak up and put a stop to this when it's going on right under your nose! I am sorry to tell you I can't stand this. It makes me too upset. You are no longer welcome to stay here unless you treat this daughter the way you treat Penny and Stephen, the way parents are supposed to treat a child. Visit if you want, but I'd better not hear a cross word to Susan when you do."

After that, we stayed at the Molly Stark motel. If Priscilla had her way, we'd never have gone back to Jesse and Willie's, but Dad the mollifier suggested the motel. He was completely smitten with Vermont, and determined to buy land of his own as soon as possible. Once he found that piece of property in nearby Marlboro, we visited Aunt Jessie and Uncle Willie a couple of times on our way through, very briefly and awkwardly, then never saw them again.

Vermont is now a way of life for the family, a weekend get-away every other week. Dad trades the sedan for a station wagon to hold all the picnics and overnight bags we pack. Priscilla takes an old pair of

Stephen's red flannel pajamas with us; Dad hangs the top from one tree along the dirt road and the bottom from another so we can easily see the boundaries of the property as we drive up. After driving three hours to get there, we spend a couple of hours walking the perimeter of the thirty acres, discovering old stone walls and what looks like bunkers used by the Green Mountain Boys. We drive all the way there to cut down our Christmas tree every year, tromping through the snow to scope out the views and the look of the woods minus their leaves.

Dad is searching for the perfect spot to site his dream house. He figures we'll build the garage first, and use that as a hard tent when we come up, until the house is built. His ideas are racing ahead so fast I crane my neck every time we get close, looking for kids my age and trying to figure out what it would be like to suddenly find myself going to school in rural Vermont. Or is this something else that doesn't concern me? Maybe they'll just leave me by myself on Marshall Road for a year or two.

An old friend has persuaded Priscilla that with her kids all in school now and her mother passed away, she can get out and kick up her heels a little. After school one day I find a note taped to the back door. "Susan. This door is locked. Go through the cellar door and up to your room. I won't be home until later." The next note will say, "Go in through the cellar." The next time the door is locked, there will be no note. Each time the house is empty. I have no idea where my siblings are; I guess Priscilla talks to them and has them make other plans ahead of time. I don't know when she's likely to come home so I stay glued to my room in case she's due any minute.

Finally I overhear enough bits and pieces of conversation to piece together that Priscilla goes to Boston on these days to have lunch with her friend and do a little shopping in the city. She gets home about an hour before dinnertime, pocketbook swinging from her hand as she walks up the street, traces of her lipstick still visible when she sits down at the dinner table. She allows her suppers on those nights to be simple affairs of reheated dishes. I allow myself to hope every day on the way home from school that the back door will be locked.

What captures Priscilla's whole-hearted attention, however, is an announcement in the paper that the town of Winchester is going to be offering a new program called "adult education." Different night courses taught by experts will be offered each semester, using classrooms at the high school. She devises a plan to sign up for the course in reupholstery, each semester bringing an old but well-made chair of Grammie's, restoring them one by one to their former glory as fine pieces of furniture. But she decides that her starting point will be an advanced sewing class. She wants to take that one first so she can make Stephen a suit and a dress coat.

The first night she is due to get out of the house and go to a class she is clearly excited. Stacked up by her dinner plate are the things she needs to bring with her: patterns, threads, needles, scissors. Intuiting what is going on from bits of overheard conversation, seeing her happy anticipation of this experience, I say to her, "Looks like you're all ready to go. I hope you enjoy the class."

"Oh, just mind your own business," she snaps back. "This doesn't concern you."

I can't help it. The tears just start flowing. I keep pushing my food around my plate, even eating it, but my head is bowed; the silent tears just won't stop dropping down the front of my sweater. I feel utterly depressed. Why am I living? What on God's green earth is the point of my existence? If there is some reason why I have to go through this, I wish someone would tell me.

Up in my room, I try to focus on homework, but I can't. Tonight it is too difficult to do anything but mull, searching for a reason why I am being made to endure this situation, why I'm expected to tolerate it, live through it, day after day after day. Why, oh why can't I make it stop? What do I have to do to make Priscilla stop this relentless harassment?

When Dad gets home from dropping off Priscilla for her class, I hear him coming upstairs. Why? Is he coming to my room? Why?

He stands in my doorway. "I want to know what it was that upset you so much at the dinner table tonight," he says.

I'm flabbergasted that he cared enough about that to come see me. At the same time, I can't believe he even needs to ask such a question. He was right there, for goodness sake! Where do I begin? "It's everything," I say. "It's that tone of voice, the way she speaks to me. I can't stand it anymore. I try to say something nice, it doesn't matter. It's all the time."

He's heard enough. "Have you done your readings for this week?" he asks.

"Some," I say.

"Look at Wednesday's passages," he says. "Particularly the one in the Science and Health." He turns away and goes back downstairs.

It's the last thing I feel like doing, but I'm curious. I look up the passage. It says, "Clad in the panoply of Love, human hatred cannot reach you." Right.

These people are so strange. Every time I start to worry about how weird I have become, I end up thinking about how strangely they are all behaving. Nevertheless, they are all free to go their own ways. I've got to go mine. That's what's been happening all my life anyway. They're just putting up with me because they have to. Year by year they know me less and less, care less and less about my experiences, my feelings, who I am, what I think, what I need. I am only a summation of their assumptions about me, which are based solely on Priscilla's irrational behavior towards me. There is no empathy here, no questioning of her authority, no effort to change the situation on my behalf. I don't belong here, never have.

We're down to the last four years; my only concern is the same as it has always been – toughing it out so I can have a life later, so that I can be normal later. I no longer think that I'll escape intact; I'm old enough now to know I'm badly wounded. But I've come this far, I can't give up. I've got to endure for four more years. I am the sole keeper of the faith, faith in Susan, faith that I am somebody, faith that if I remember what is happening to me, someday I will be able to tell the story.

"You have your memory," I tell myself for the umpteenth time. "No one can take that away. Remember everything."

Epilogues

Lorraine, Susan; 1963

Lorraine

"I've been planning this for a long, long time," Lorraine said. I sat beside her in the front seat of her car, stunned by my good fortune. "Scoot over here right next to me," she said, picking up her big black handbag and dumping it on my lap. She'd come up for Penny's high school graduation the day before, when I knew nothing of her plan and thought I'd be doomed to haunting the tennis courts all summer. But that morning over breakfast, in front of the entire family, Lorraine invited me to come back to Greenwich with her. I couldn't pack fast enough.

"That's why I took your sister last summer." Lorraine's face beamed as she drove towards the highway, one hand on the wheel, one hand holding mine. Penny had spent the previous summer in Greenwich, working for Lorraine, building up her secretarial credentials with a full-time office position in Lorraine's business. I thought my parents set that up to give Penny the extra advantages they had always given her. Instead, Lorraine was telling me she dreamed up the whole idea. "I wanted to make sure your parents would agree to this," Lorraine said, "so I took Penny first. I've been talking to them about it for two years."

I was still trying to grasp the reality: here I was, beside Lorraine, in the beloved two-toned Ford sedan, on my way to spend the entire summer with her. "I don't know much about being a secretary," I said, reminding her that she was getting a poor deal, someone who had no mind for shorthand and bookkeeping. "I'm going to be taking a class in touch typing next year," I added, not wanting to come across as totally helpless, hopeless, useless. "It's required for the college-bound program. Right now, though, I can't type for beans."

"That's alright, Sweetie," said Lorraine, squeezing my hand. "You aren't going to be working for me. I did that with Penny so your parents would go along with the idea of taking you this summer. You're going to stay in the apartment or walk around town and do whatever you want to while I'm at the office. When I'm not working, we'll do things together. Since my office is in the same building, you can come down and visit if you need some company. It might be a little hard on you, to be by yourself all day, but we'll have lots of time together."

"I'm used to being by myself," I said. "My mother makes me stay by myself all the time." I wanted right then to tell Aunt Lorraine everything that Priscilla did to me. It would have been such a relief to let her know the all of it. The weight of it was threatening to crush me, knowing I finally had the right person to tell, all to myself, right beside me. But Lorraine let me know she wanted none of that.

"Listen, Sweetie. You can spend your summer dwelling on all that and feeling miserable, or you can just leave it behind and enjoy this experience. It would be a shame to waste our time together complaining about your situation, wouldn't it? Wouldn't you rather have a good time?" Chagrinned, I saw her point.

For the next ten weeks, she loved me to pieces and spoiled me rotten. We went to Broadway plays, the Shakespearian theater up the coast in Stratford, Lindy's diner in New York City, Chinese tea rooms and other fancy ethnic restaurants. Occasionally I sat in on business meetings that took place over dinners in Manhattan. Swearing me to secrecy, she brought me along to the country club on one of her lunch dates with an elderly married man who loved having her vivacious company now and then. When she gave cocktail parties, she included handsome young men my age. I wore new clothes Lorraine bought for me, along with makeup, perfume and one of her large jade rings – her present to me on my sixteenth birthday that summer. Everyone thought we were mother and daughter. We dressed to accentuate the look – me, by stuffing my bras with tissues to poof up my chest; Lorraine, by buying me swishy dresses in her favorite turquoise hues and letting me wear strings of her pearls.

Whenever Lorraine could get the time, we went to the beach. She loved the water and taught me how to do the side stroke, although I still wouldn't go out over my head. She also got tremendous enjoyment out of going to Yonkers and Roosevelt raceways; we dined in their club houses often, rubbing elbows with many of her clients from the city. She bet only on horses with Scottish names and never left with losses. Once in a while we cooked a meal at home, exploring different ways to use the "ground round, ground twice" that she'd have me pick up for her at Gristedes. Her specialty, though, was veal marsala, with lady fingers for dessert.

More than the introduction to her healthy, happy, ritzy grown-up world, more than the lessons in manners and social graces, Lorraine taught me pleasant ways of dealing with people. Every individual she encountered – waiters, close friends, office staff, residents of the apartment building, shopkeepers – experienced her genuine warmth and attentive respect. She started teaching me how to interact with people from the moment we went through our first toll booth on the Merritt Parkway during the drive back to Greenwich.

She stopped long enough to have a casual conversation with the toll collector about the weather and the traffic, gave him some of her winsome smiles and her throaty chuckles. As we pulled away I asked, "Do you know him because you drive this road a lot?"

"No, I don't know him," she said. "Look, Sweetie. It doesn't hurt to talk to people. When someone has a service job you should go out of your way to be pleasant to them. It seems to me it's all the more important to take a moment to be friendly to these people, let them know you see a human being, not a machine. Everyone enjoys a little light conversation. It makes the day go a lot faster, brings some relief to the boredom." In other words, we're all equals and deserve to be treated as such. In her, that idea was more than a moral stance; it was ingrained down to her very soul, expressed unequivocally. I spent the summer paying attention to her, to what made her so fabulous, wanting with all my heart to be like her.

We talked as I imagined mothers and daughters talked, often lounging on her king-sized bed at night, Lorraine stripped down to her slip with the air conditioner cranking away, her two Siamese cats frolicking around us. She discussed with me the importance of getting a part-time job when I returned home, the need to start earning my own money and saving for things I needed. My parents would expect to get a portion of my pay every week for my "room and board," but I'd have money left to save and a little to spend. The key word in these talks was independence.

Lorraine was excited about my plans to go to college and be a teacher. Priscilla had told me I needed to confine my college applications to state teachers colleges, so Lorraine and I made a pact that I would apply to Danbury, which was less than an hour from Greenwich, and we would be a family from then on. In those days, you had to teach in the same state where you had gotten your teaching degree.

But Priscilla had other ideas. "You'll go to a college in this state," she said flatly when the time came to fill out applications that fall. "You're father and I aren't paying out-of-state tuition for you. It costs an arm and a leg as it is to go to one of the in-state colleges." It broke my heart.

Lorraine was philosophical about it. "We'll figure it out," she said. "You might be able to teach in Connecticut if you can take a couple of extra courses down here in the summers. It might take a little longer, but good things are worth waiting for, right Sweetie?"

Ironically, the Massachusetts college that accepted me notified me at the last minute that I would not be able to live on campus because I lived close enough to commute. Neither Priscilla nor I could stand the thought of another four years at home, so the search began for another teacher's college I could attend. There were none in Massachusetts that still had openings for the fall semester, none in Connecticut either. The only teacher's colleges that were still accepting applicants at that late date were located in remote regions of northern New England, so I ended up getting my degree in New Hampshire, a seven hour drive away from Lorraine. It changed everything.

During that summer in Greenwich, however, I assumed that once I got through high school, the rest of my life would be lived by Lorraine's side. I finally had a clear post-Priscilla plan. I soaked up every moment of that delicious idyll, storing the love and delight, the laughter and intimacy with Lorraine, so that I could make it through my last two years at home. I was loved, and I was very nearly free.

Time After Time

During the days, I watched a lot of TV, catching up on cartoons, Lucy and Gunsmoke, Sid Caesar and Jackie Gleason and other shows I'd never seen that were now on as reruns. I read Lorraine's collection of Thomas Costain historical novels and hung out with her Jamaican maid Mary watching the Loretta Young show. I read the New York Times every day as part of working my way through a book Lorraine gave me called It Pays to Increase Your Word Power. I sunned myself on the roof of the building by day, drank ginger ale floats every night and gained 40 pounds that would melt away as soon as I got back home.

Two years later, on the morning of my high school graduation, Lorraine awoke with a pain in her right arm. She looked gorgeous, as always, in pearls and a turquoise linen dress that matched her new turquois and white Ford sedan. But as the day wore on the pain spread to her torso, became worse and worse, dimming her spark, supplanting it with worry. "I wonder if the surgeon left something in there when I had that hysterectomy a couple of months ago," she said, unable to pinpoint what was going on, unfamiliar with this level of discomfort. She left earlier than planned to go home and see her doctor.

Within a year she was so disabled by multiple sclerosis she had to sell her business. For the first time in her life, money was tight. She took in typing jobs at home, got a Marymount college student to rent the second bedroom and bath in her apartment, rarely dressed up or had her hair done. Nevertheless, she continued to be my rock and my champion.

The fact that my parents had agreed to let me be with Lorraine for that summer made it easy to arrange get-aways from then on. Going home for a holiday or a school break meant going to Greenwich. I took the train from Boston, smoking and hanging out en route with the boys going to and from the Norwich Naval Academy. Lorraine would have a pile of clothes ready for me to try on – dresses that that she had selected with one of the shopkeepers in town, or good wool skirts she had saved from her days as a pencil-thin young lady. We went through her shoe closet to see if there were any that fit. "Never throw your shoes away," she said. "They always come back in style." When she found out I had a date for the formal dance during junior weekend in college, she bought my gown and sent it to me along with her blue fox cape and long white gloves. Inside the fur she had tucked one of her beaded purses, and inside its tiny pocket she stuck a card that said, "Dearest Love. Have fun. Lorraine."

One bitter cold New Year's Eve Lorraine and I were dressing for a party at the hotel near her apartment: me in a sleeveless red velvet dress she had bought for me that had white pearls gathered into the fabric, she in a flowing black evening gown with a turquoise silk shawl. She brought me the blue fox cape to wear. "Isn't it too cold for that?" I said. "It only covers my shoulders."

"Sometimes," she said grinning, "you have to wear your pride higher than your ass."

My father got his first brand new car when I was in college. He put the initial break-in miles on it by driving Priscilla down to Greenwich on a Friday to deliver her for a weekend visit with Lorraine, then driving back home. On Saturday, he and Stephen arrived unannounced in the lobby of my dorm for a quick visit, a three-hour drive in the opposite direction. On Sunday, they drove back to Greenwich to pick up Priscilla. Lorraine called me that Sunday night.

"It was just the two of us. I think she had a good time. She seemed happy to be here. So listen, Sweetie. One night I tried to talk to your mother about the way she is with you. She had just had a glass of wine; your mother likes a glass of wine now and then, you know. I could tell she was relaxed. So I asked her, 'Why do you treat Susan the way you do?'

"She said, 'I don't know.' Just like that. It seemed genuine. Like she really doesn't know."

Lorraine was an astute reader of people's feelings, so I believed in the authenticity of Priscilla's response, blessed Lorraine for trying to get me an answer. The answer. She was the only one who ever dared to ask point blank like that. I'm sure she looked at Priscilla in respectful silence for a few moments, waiting to see if anything more would come out, but nothing did.

"You know," she said, "your mother is at heart a very good person. She was telling me about having to take that old dog, Dini, that they've had for a couple of years to see the vet. Oh! I'm going to cry when I tell you this. It made me cry when she told me and it still makes me cry." She paused. "The vet said it was time to put Dini to sleep. And he told your mother that it would be nice for Dini if someone was with her and petted her while she was dying." Lorraine stopped, her crying audible. "So she did." She stopped again for a moment. "Your mother went in there and stroked Dini's head until she died."

After a few minutes to recover, Lorraine said, "I could never do that. She is so dispassionate, and that is not a bad way to be. I wish I could be like that sometimes."

Lorraine moved to Scottsdale, Arizona my first year of teaching. She'd been wrestling with the decision for over a year. The cost of living there was much less than it was in Greenwich, she said; the dry desert air was supposed to be good for people with her condition. One of her former husbands lived in Sedona and had helped her to find a house. He kept an eye on her now and then. But it continued to be a meager life for this high-spirited woman who used to draw people to her like a magnet with the power of her personality.

Lorraine died alone in Scottsdale when I was 28 years old, long, long before I was healed enough to figure out how to move there and teach there and tend her like a daughter.

Ed; Hingham, 1967

Ed

The congregation of the Winchester Christian Science church finally grew large enough to consider having a church of their own instead of renting the Knights of Columbus Hall downtown. Dad volunteered to be part of the building committee, and once the church was finally under construction, he drove us to the building site every week or so to admire the emerging structure he had helped to design and fund. It became a beautiful white-spired New England style church set on an open corner lot on a broad street full of Victorian houses and shady trees.

Immediately, the congregation elected Dad to be the first First Reader in the new building, a position that carried a three-year commitment. Thrilled by the unexpected honor, he put his Vermont dreams on hold. His face beamed with joy at his new stature within the church. He added expensive suits to his wardrobe, suits he wore to lead the Sunday services. These included a specially tailored white flannel suit that is the traditional Sunday outfit for a First Reader during the summer months. He had rarely attended the Wednesday night "testimonial" services before his election, but for those three years he was there every week.

At home, the dining room displayed a new dictionary stand with an Oxford English Dictionary. Dad used that and his new Concordance to the Bible to review the passages he and the Second Reader would read to the congregation that week. Mary Baker Eddy's often obscure vocabulary required that kind of intense study. Priscilla was his devoted help mate, even with her disdain for Christian Science. Each night after supper, positioned in her chair across from his desk in the den, her needlepoint or sewing in her lap, she stopped as needed, looked up words in the dictionary for him, helped him pronounce words and listened to him read the week's passages aloud until he could say them smoothly and put the emphasis in the right places.

One Sunday he was silent as a stone all the way home from the service. He went up to his room to change out of his suit without his usual conversation with Priscilla on the way through the kitchen. Finally we all sat at the dinner table and he stood to carve the roast. Priscilla asked, "So how did the service go today, Dear?"

"Oh, I flubbed those three words," he said, and completely broke down in tears. He fled to the bathroom and shut the door. Priscilla wasted no time, took her napkin off her lap, put it by her plate, got up and went to him. The sound of him weeping gut-wrenching tears was awful. I started crying. This was the only time we three kids saw our father cry, and it was because he flubbed three words when reading to his congregation. We had two parents who were perfectionists.

I could hear Priscilla talking him through it, soothing him. She came back to the table alone while he composed himself. "What are you crying for?" she snapped at me. "This doesn't concern you." Then, looking at all of us she said, "You three kids mind your own business now. Don't say a word to your father. This is none of your affair." When he came back to the table, he carved the roast in a deafening silence, eyes rimmed with that red stain that says how raw the wound inside.

Normally Dad was so fluent at seeing everyone and everything as perfect, years would pass between events that tossed him around like that, things that took him a little extra time and thought to process through the Christina Science lens. When I was a freshman in college he sent me a private note that indicated he was having one of those challenges to his thinking. "Your mother found the letter you wrote to Janice when you were home for Thanksgiving," he said. Priscilla had taken pieces of a ripped up letter out of my wastebasket, put them together like a jigsaw puzzle and showed them to Dad to complain about my attitude. I could just imagine how that conversation went, something like, "Why are we paying an arm and a leg to send *That One* to college when all she can do is complain about what we do for her?"

But something in those tattered words had gotten through to Dad enough for him to write to me. "I want to know why you were so upset. If you write back, send your letter to my office. This is just between us, not something you need to mention to your mother."

I could picture Dad composing the letter at his office desk. I had stopped by there one day when I was in Boston, a teen-aged waif wandering around the city because her mother had told her, bluntly and without direction, that she was old enough to go into town and buy her own clothes. Dad's company was on the 14th floor of the Herald Traveller's office building. When he came out to the reception area to get me and walk me back to his office that day, I was stunned by the difference between that office and the room he had taken me to on a Saturday when I was five years old.

He had become the chief financial officer of the company, had a corner office with floor to ceiling windows on two sides, one side of which had a breath-taking view of Boston Harbor. On his desk, a single document sat square in the center, his elegant pen angled across it. No photos of his family anywhere, no decorations. Stark. His desk was positioned a good bit towards the middle of the large room, away from the windows, facing away from any view. Fear of heights. From the chair I sat in facing his desk, I was the one who got the view of sailboats on a sparkling blue sea.

Getting a letter with his office as the return address was a shocker. I was incredulous that Dad would keep anything from Priscilla. At the same time, I found myself thinking, "Here we go again. I have to explain to my father how painful it is to be his daughter. He cannot understand what it was like to go home for the first time in 12 weeks and be met with the same animosity from Priscilla, the same confinement to my room, the same utter lack of tolerance for my presence in the family." He remained blind to it all. The thought that I could be upset with my visit home had disturbed his normally unshakable conviction that everything was harmonious and good.

Had that same Christian Science framework of beliefs turned me into a Pollyanna? Why else did I continue to hope that things would get better? Stupidly, somewhere along the way I had fallen into the trap of thinking that time would be the healer; the longer I stayed away, the greater the chances of being welcome upon my return. Three weeks with Uncle Bud and Auntie Belle weren't enough when I was 10; let's try three months away at college.

But nothing had changed. Priscilla didn't even say hello. Thanksgiving was just another day in the life I lived in that house. In a moment of despair I had tried to explain my feelings in a letter to my best friend from high school, only to realize that even Janice wouldn't want to hear about the angst that I still couldn't handle. I already had friends in the dorm telling me I needed to stop talking about Priscilla all the time; they were tired of listening and didn't believe half of it anyway. So I had ripped the aborted letter to pieces and licked my wounds in silence.

Then Dad's letter came, giving me a big, wide open door for talking to him about my situation. I spent the entire weekend sitting cross-legged on my bed in the quiet dorm, writing my response to him on yellow lined paper. I tried to tell him everything, tried to shock him with details that would finally penetrate that Christian Science shield of his. The letter was 13 pages long, the result of a well-cultivated memory. I revealed to him the extent to which Priscilla's venomous attitude and behavior had been out of control, over the years and beyond his ken. The board spankings, the "I hate you," the black and blues, the hours spent down cellar scrubbing clothes in the set tubs. What I tried hardest to convey, though, was how deeply it hurt to be treated differently, day after day, year after year; to have suffered through the blatant animosity and so many ways of being shunned and excluded from family life, for no reason. I wanted him to understand the all of it, except for its apparently permanent effect on my elimination system. That was too delicate, something that made me feel shame, as if I were to blame. I hid that painful issue from everyone, knowing how freakish it made me.

"Your mother loves you," he wrote back, simplifying everything into the only terms that mattered to him. "She has always worked hard to be a good mother to you three kids. You need to practice what your church has taught you. We will not speak of this again."

Not long afterward, Lorraine said in a phone call. "You mother says your father is slowing down a lot."

"What does that mean?" I wanted to know, fear of the unknown gripping me. Wasn't that something that happened to old people? Dad was in his late forties.

"He's just not doing as much," she said. "Doesn't seem to have much energy."

They sold the property in Vermont when I was a sophomore. A year later they moved to a 3-bedroom ranch house in Hingham, back on the South Shore. The move was prompted in part by wanting to get Stephen into a regional vocational school because he wasn't doing well in the academically competitive Winchester schools. But the main emphasis was on downsizing, having less of a house to care for, now that their family consisted of only one child living at home, now that Dad was slowing down.

Dad met me in Boston, when I came home for Christmas, so that we could take trains and buses to Hingham together; I had never been to the new house. He was so subdued on the ride home I couldn't get a conversation going. He seemed smaller, physically and mentally run down, a man low on both words and energy who sat a little slumped in his seat, looking out the window at the city lights flashing by. Knowing him, I assumed his mind was taking the lion's share of his attention, working and working to make sure his all-good world was put to rights because something was threatening to knock it out of kilter.

After that holiday season, he started getting sick. At first it was described as "a cold he just couldn't shake." This man who couldn't bear to step on a ladder or look out his office windows worked with a Christian Science practitioner so that he could steel himself to take his first plane trip. He and Priscilla and Stephen went to Florida for a week to see if that would "bake the chest cold out of him." It didn't.

By springtime he was so sick he had to take a leave of absence from work. The upper respiratory infection irritated his lungs so much that eventually he couldn't speak; trying to talk made him choke. He had a high fever, was often delirious. He would not go to a doctor. A Christian Science practitioner came to the house every day to read and pray with him.

His physical ailments meant he could not come to my college graduation. He made Penny and Priscilla come, leaving Stephen at home to care for him while Priscilla seethed with fury at being forced to leave his side to go to something she had absolutely no interest in. Dad made sure, though, that Uncle Ralph would stand in for him – not just by taking a lot of photographs of the event but by bringing his family to spend the day with me, to make me feel that I had family there. He knew that Penny and Priscilla wouldn't spend one iota of time or energy beyond showing up.

I called Dad after all the guests had left that night. Penny answered the phone.

"I want to talk to Dad," I said.

"Well, he can't talk," she said. "It makes him choke."

"That's OK," I said. "I'll do the talking. Please see if he'll come to the phone."

Again, Penny balked at the idea, but Dad had caught on by then that I was the one calling. "OK. He's coming to the phone. But keep it short. He shouldn't be doing this."

"Buh!" A choked word from Dad.

"Hi, Dad. Don't try to talk, OK? I just wanted to thank you for everything. I was sorry you couldn't be there today. I missed you, and wanted you to know how grateful I am for my college education."

Cough. Wheeze.

"It was a beautiful day for it, which is good because it was all done outside on the lawn of the dorm."

"Rmph! Buh!"

"Uncle Ralph and his family were here all day. They came up early and visited for quite a while before the graduation and then came back to the house afterward for the party. He took lots and lots of pictures, Dad, so you'll be able to see it all. It was a great day."

"Gmph."

"OK, Dad. I don't want to keep you. Take good care. I'll see you soon."

"Bumph. Gomph." Sounds coughed out under the strain of trying not to choke.

Dad lost over 100 pounds during his illness. His hair and eyebrows turned completely white. Priscilla was wearing herself out again, this time caring for someone who refused medical attention, so there was no back-up for her, no relief. At one point that summer, he was delirious for 4 days straight. When a lucid moment finally came, Priscilla convinced him to let her call an ambulance, telling him she could no longer take care of him. The minute the EMTs put the oxygen mask on him he felt better. "Put the siren on!" he exclaimed, like a little kid. "I want to hear the siren!"

While he was hospitalized, he made Priscilla write to me every other week, as he himself had done all during my college years. "Your father had me write this," the letters began. "Your father says," she prefaced everything. And when she finally relented to my pleas to come see him, she made it an order. "You get yourself down here and visit your father!" As if she hadn't been denying my request for weeks. I nearly fainted when I saw him – that frail, old man with the white hair and eyebrows laying prone on the bed, with barely enough energy for talking.

He did recover. He went back to work part-time in the fall, and got into the habit of doing daily walks around the neighborhood, with its long views of the sailboats in Hingham Harbor. Inevitably, though, he stopped taking his medicine and resumed his total reliance on Christian Science. When I went to see him at Christmas, he was on leave from work again. We talked for less than an hour, then Priscilla herded him off to bed to rest.

He was back in the hospital in January, in intensive care. Uncle Ralph stood alone at his bedside one day; Priscilla had gone home for a bit of a rest. "You'll talk to Susan?" Dad said to his brother.

"I will," said Uncle Ralph. Then the ICU machines bleeped and whirred and erupted into a frenzy indicating massive organ failure. Dad was dead, at the age of 52. "I took those words to mean that he wanted me to look after you, you know what I mean?" said Uncle Ralph. "He knew damn well Pete would just close you out."

I had a dream a few years later. In it, my father appeared as a wholly spiritual being. He had a white and holy aura as he strode from one side of a large living room to the other to sit in a wing-backed chair by the fireplace. Dressed in a typical white shirt, red bow tie and dark suit pants, he seemed much more trim and fit than he was in the prime of his life. He was completely whole, completely healthy, in a way that surpassed human experience. He had left mortal bounds to exist in a state of utter well-being and intense spiritual existence. I was a spectator in the dream, standing by the near wall. I sensed that he had come back to accomplish something; he could not move on as a spiritual being until he resolved an important issue.

As he sat in the chair, my mother appeared in the room and stood before him. Off to the right, a screen porch extended out from the far wall. All of my mother's family was sitting around a picnic table out there: Uncle Bud, Aunt Wilma, Auntie Belle, and other shadowy figures I couldn't identify clearly, perhaps her mother and father, aunts and uncles, others who had passed on. The table was crowded with them.

My father, without saying a word, gave my mother to understand that she must go out to the porch and talk to these people. She was to talk about why she had been so awful to me, had to discuss it honestly and fully with her family and stay out there until she understood everything. He let her know that her family would be supportive and caring throughout and would help her to find the essential truth.

She went out to the porch. I watched from my vantage point along the wall she sat surrounded by her family. They put all their heads together over the table to help my mother to do the painful inner work needed to grapple with this problem. It took a long, long time.

Eventually, she came out, exhausted but at peace with herself. Again at my father's unspoken insistence, she was given to understand that she had to approach me for the final resolution. She walked over to me, still reluctant but knowing she must, and gave me a hug around the waist, her head leaning softly on my chest. I was flooded with warmth and love for her, and for myself.

So Dad came back to give me this: the answer was within her family, and some unnamed pain she experienced there.

Priscilla; Hingham, 1969

Priscilla

Priscilla became a widow at the age of 53. While a team of nurses and doctors removed the tubes and equipment from Dad's body, wiped down the room and tidied up, Priscilla soldiered on, thinking about phone calls and arrangements to be made. "I'll call Susan," Uncle Ralph said to her.

"Well she's not staying with me!" Priscilla said, vehement. "I haven't got room. I'll have Penny and Belle and Donnie."

"That's alright," Uncle Ralph said. "She can stay with us."

"Well then, you'll have to choose. It's her or me," Priscilla said, turning her back and walking away.

With Dad gone, she no longer had any reason to continue suffering through marginal accommodations of my presence in her family. That was it. She was done, free to exclude me to her heart's content. The one-time boarder could be eliminated from her life, no ties whatsoever. She put herself, Penny and Stephen into a receiving line at the wake, sat separately with them at the funeral and spoke not a word to me.

Lorraine couldn't make it to Dad's funeral but she flew back from Arizona the next Christmas, insisting that we all get together in Hingham for the holiday, forcing Priscilla to put up with my presence. However, it had become impossible for me to tolerate my mother's overt shunning and animosity by then. I was in my second year of teaching, used to living alone, and by then I had a choice. So, after my ancient car had been sitting at Priscilla's house in below zero temperatures for four days, I went out early in the morning and marshaled every trick I knew for getting the engine to start. The only thing that worked was will power.

The sheer force of my determination to get out of there must have moved heaven and earth; on the fourth try, the engine finally kicked over and caught, making the decision easy. Even though Lorraine would still be there, I was leaving.

I stood right by Priscilla's elbow in the kitchen and told her the news quietly as she buttered toast for breakfast. It surprised her into speaking to me.

"I thought you were staying for the rest of the week!"

"I was, but I can't."

"I know," she said, relieved. "Okay then."

Whenever I tried a phone call after that, Priscilla hung up as soon as I said my name. When I wrote, she ignored the letter. I waited a year, then two years, then five years between attempts, ever the optimist that time would be a healer, but to no avail.

One year I drove for three hours to deliver Christmas presents for her and the family, hoping that if I came unannounced I could get at least a few minutes of normal conversation with her. She opened the front door, noted the pile of wrapped gifts, with a wave of her arm said, "You can put them there on the couch," held the door open until I left and shut it behind me. No hello, no good-by.

Another time, on the advice of a friend who did crisis counseling and thought I should treat Priscilla as you would someone who was suicidal, I wrote that I would "be in town" on a certain date , and would like to "stop by for a cup of coffee" at a certain time in the afternoon "for just a few minutes." She opened that letter, I know, because she wrote back to say she had other plans that day and wouldn't be home. When I wrote back calmly suggesting another day and time, her response was venomous.

"I've managed to make a new life for myself these past few years without any help from you!" she wrote angrily, "and I don't need your help now! I have nothing to say to you!"

Priscilla had gotten her driver's license just before the move to Hingham, so she had a level of independence that she hadn't had in Winchester. She stayed at home for a couple of years, until Stephen graduated from high school, then she got a full-time job as an executive secretary. She did not retire from that position until she was 83 years old; she was considered indispensable to her boss.

She had a couple of friends from work that she saw socially from time to time, but in general she continued being the epitome of a homemaker. She added a deck to the house, painted woodwork, put up new wallpaper, redecorated rooms. She sewed curtains, knitted afghans, did crochet and needlepoint. Once in a blue moon she'd mention my name to Auntie Belle or Uncle Bud. "I suppose Susan's married by now?" And they'd tell her briefly what I was doing.

In her sixties, she had an operation to remove a cancerous uterus. She also became diabetic, and had to start closely monitoring her weight and her blood sugar. In her seventies, she had a pacemaker to regulate her heartbeat. She began wearing glasses as her eyesight deteriorated from macular degeneration, a condition related to her diabetes.

By the time she finally retired, her health had failed so much that she had to give up driving. A couple of times, when Penny or neighbors called to check on her, they got no answer; she had fallen on the floor and couldn't move. One day as she walked out to the curb in front of the house to meet the senior van that took her to medical appointments, she tripped and injured her foot. She went into a nursing home for rehabilitation. Almost totally blind by then, the doctors told her that she wasn't going to be able to live independently at home any more. She died in the nursing home a few weeks later, at the age of 86.

Once again, it was Uncle Ralph who called. "Are you going to go to the funeral?" I asked him.

"I'm too angry," he said. "I am so angry at all the things she's done to you! I say good riddance to bad rubbish. I wouldn't pay my respects to her if you gave me a million dollars. I'd probably try to strangle the body if I went there."

At the funeral parlor, I sat alone for a few moments in the room where Priscilla's open coffin lay, tried to take in the sight of her old woman self. She had on a beautiful blue silk dress, and the large diamond Dad had given her on their 20th anniversary. Giant glasses dominated her unrecognizable face. The more I tried to compose some prayerful thoughts, the more I swore her body was moving, trying desperately to get out of the coffin and come after me. The feeling that her animosity was still alive and present was so real I had to leave the room.

The minister met with we three kids before the service. "Is there a favorite Bible passage you would like me to read?"

"She wasn't a very religious person," Penny said.

"What were her favorite things?" the minister asked.

"She was a simple woman," Penny said crossly. "She worked up until three years ago. She liked her house and her handwork. She liked to cook and sew." No mention of kids, grandkids, family.

One of her friends from work was at the funeral. "I'm so glad to meet you," she said to me, peering closely at my face. "I knew about you. You look like her." Then after a pause, "One time your mother said to me out of the blue, 'I have another daughter, too, but I don't know what her name is or where she lives.' I didn't push," the friend said. "The way we were brought up, people told you what they wanted to tell you and it was up to them if they wanted to tell you more. That was all she ever said about it."

"She did such beautiful handwork," her friend went on tearfully. "She made these lovely afghans and gave them away to people. You should see them! I have the most gorgeous one she made for me, all white. I treasure it. She gave another friend of ours one that had beautiful violets crocheted all over it. Oh, she did such lovely work!"

As I was leaving the funeral, that same woman came up behind me, weeping as she tapped me on the shoulder. She reached into her purse and pulled out a photo. "This was taken at her retirement party," she said. "Would you like to have it?" In the photo, Priscilla sits like a queen in a chair surrounded by her good friends from work, wearing a pink dress and the same huge glasses she had on in her coffin. Her cane hangs over the end of her chair. Her complexion is mottled with age spots, but her smile is as big as the crepe paper loops decorating the walls behind her. My mother.

Once I began to write down the story of my childhood in its entirety, my dreams were often peopled with family characters, Priscilla most of all. We talked in dreams, we shopped and cooked together, we hugged, we lived in sweet harmony in our house, usually the one on Marshall Road. Dreams provided resolution, making everything turn out right, the way I wished it had been.

In one especially healing dream, I was standing in a cafeteria line with my tray, surrounded by colleagues and friends who were all women, all beloved. We smiled and talked. Something full of meaning was about to happen – a culmination, a ritual, a show. We were the reason for it. We had achieved something awesome and fine. It was the kind of event to which one invites the near and dear. "Come see me. See what I can do, what I am." Everyone was happily anticipating the arrival of loved ones to share the moment.

I was serene and joyful in the company of those women. Surrounded by their love and good will, secure in my adult maturity, a part of me realized that I was nonetheless steeling myself for a predictable disappointment. She would not come. "Everyone else's mother will be here," I tried explaining to someone in my middle-aged, matter-of-fact voice. "I will look around only to verify what I already know. Mine would never show up for this, for me."

I was certain of this at last. That was new. In times past, I harbored unreasonable, too-conscious hope that my mother would be there to witness events that felt like major accomplishments. See how worthy I have become! Look at the additional talents and qualities I have developed! I shall pile them one on top of another until they reach the sky! I shall paste layer upon layer onto my person until the universe is filled with my remarkable presence! Then you shall see me! But I knew, finally, with a conviction born of ineradicable scars: my mother would not come because she did not care. She would not see me no matter how wondrous the sight. She would rather pluck out her eyes.

I turned from these thoughts to move my tray down the cafeteria line, and there she was! She was in a group of visitors walking in from behind the counter to join us. I experienced the flood of elation that was the gift of every dream I had with this theme of reconciliation with Priscilla. It was as if everything that had been thought, felt and done between my mother and me went into a body blender, the puree button was pressed, and when it all calmed down, it had been transformed into the ultimate soul-filling elixir.

I was thrilled. She came. She did not look like Priscilla in this dream; she was a youthful, healthy-looking older woman with long salt-and-pepper hair and buck teeth, wearing a casual, unbelted denim jumper. I knew her, though. She had been in my dreams before. She was very dear. She was my mother. The eye contact was good. She wanted to shrug it off as no big deal. I wouldn't let her.

"Dance with me," I said. "You must dance with me. That's what this is all about. It will heal us. You came, and that is wonderful. Now dance with me. I need to dance with you. Please."

She did, disjointed and shy, but with the best of intentions. Pure joy was mine in that instant before I woke up.

Stephen and daughters

Stephen

By the time Stephen was old enough to think about his family in the abstract and wonder why there was this oddity of a sister who wasn't allowed to do anything, I was in junior high. The difference in our status in the family was compounded by the difference in our ages. And yet, Stephen figured out that he could have a relationship with me – as long as no one was looking. When he was a child, those opportunities were few and far between, occurring mainly if he happened to come upstairs to his room at a time when everyone else was downstairs.

Our rooms were on diagonally opposite corners of the house. "Psst," he'd signal from his doorway. When I appeared in mine, he'd waggle his hand to show me he had a balsa airplane or some other silent missile before he launched it across the open stairwell that yawned between us. Always there was the threat of Priscilla catching onto the furtive sounds we made. When she did, she marched into the downstairs hallway and called up harshly, "Stephen. You stay away from her. One of her is bad enough."

Otherwise, Stephen and I chatted at church on Sundays, especially when Dad became First Reader. We three kids arrived early with him, getting there at least a half hour before anyone else. Dad immediately retired to his little study behind the pulpit area. Penny went downstairs to sit at the table her Sunday School class used, waiting for others in her age group to arrive. Stephen and I wandered the building and the grounds, hanging out together like brother and sister until precisely 11 minutes before the hour. That's when Dad wanted us upstairs to stand at the doors he and the Second Reader used to walk out to their pulpits. At precisely 10 minutes before the hour, and at precisely the same time, Stephen would open the Second Reader's door while I opened Dad's, and then we'd softly close the doors behind them after they had walked out together.

Stephen's life as a teenager was like that of an only child: Penny was working in Washington, D.C.; I was away at college. Once I happened to call home when our parents weren't around. He told me that he was taking trombone lessons, that he was using my viola as a guitar and wishing he could play guitar instead of trombone, that he was friends with a girl whose brother I had been close to. But after the move to Hingham, the shared and familiar references didn't exist anymore. He was just 16 when Dad had his horribly ill year, 17 when he died.

Stephen lived at home for another ten years. It was hard for him to consider striking out on his own, leaving his widowed mother alone to mow the lawn and shovel the snow. Unbeknownst to Priscilla, though, he took a day off from work one time in order to drive to New Hampshire and look me up. Since he came unannounced, I was away that day and had no idea about his plan until I got home and found his note.

When Priscilla left for a week to visit Lorraine in Scottsdale by herself, Stephen called me to see if we could arrange a visit in Hingham. He had a thorough grasp on his mother's attitude: having a relationship with me would result in falling completely out of her good graces. "You can't park at the house," he said. "The neighbors would tell her a car with New Hampshire plates was here. Come to the store where I work and meet me there." So that's what we did, and because we couldn't go home and sit down for a nice chat, we drove around Hingham for hours.

Years passed before we connected again. I heard through aunts and uncles that Stephen was serious about a woman who had a three-year-old daughter, that he married her. His wife got in touch with me, sending a long letter full of curiosity about why my mother had no contact with me. What was the situation that Stephen found so hard to explain? She enclosed some photographs of their family.

In his late 30's then, Stephen looked exactly like Dad at that age, right down to the balding head of brown hair. The photos made it clear that he loved having a family and being a father. He called soon afterward to tell me they were having a baby. "Do you want this child to know her Aunt Susan?" I asked him.

"Yes, I do," he said firmly. When photos of the baby came, they showed a girl who looked eerily like Penny. It took a couple of years to work out our visit, but finally we got together for an awkward afternoon at his apartment. An array of gadgets, computers and stereo systems lined his living room walls, testifying to his career in electronics. His daughters were lively and full of smiles. The two-year-old was especially attached to Stephen.

So much time had passed, so much had happened in each of our lives. Stephen had been diagnosed with Hodgkins disease. He was gaunt and bald from chemotherapy. I shared with him a family photo album I'd put together from pictures relatives had given me over the years. He pored over it for a long, long time.

"I have another aunt," said the oldest girl as she sat beside me at the lunch table. "Aunt Penny."

And right there in front of us was the impossibility of continuing the relationship. Suppose one of the girls said to Priscilla or Penny, "I have an Aunt Susan." Priscilla had helped Stephen out from time to time, especially when his illness led to loss of work and trouble meeting his bills. For the sake of his own family now, he needed to maintain a positive relationship with Priscilla. His girls already considered Aunt Penny an important relative. Their holidays always included visits with Priscilla and Penny in Hingham. There was no way the character "Aunt Susan" could enter and depart from their family like a cameo role in a movie.

Our lives returned to the familiar lack of contact. One day Stephen stopped by a cousin's floral shop to announce that he and his wife had had a baby boy. Our cousin, Uncle Ralph's daughter, encouraged Stephen to bring his family to her house for a visit someday. Eventually, with our cousin acting as the intermediary, we all worked out a date when I would be visiting Uncle Ralph and Stephen could bring his family to the cousin's house and we would all meet up there for brunch. By then his son was two years old, his daughters six and nine.

He looked robust again, a tall, beefy man so like our Dad in appearance and mannerisms. A taciturn man like Dad, projecting shyness, wearing shaded glasses as the result of an eye condition. We barely spoke, focusing instead on the three lively children around us and the conversation among everyone at the table. He held his children, comforted them, got them in and out of jackets, in and out of car seats. I took pictures.

The next time we saw each other was several years later at Priscilla's funeral. Stephen had just taken a job in California. The move seemed to energize him. He was trim and fit, involved in cub scouts with his son, going on overnight hikes with the troop. The fresh start freed him from living in Priscilla's geographical vicinity, where he had had to deal regularly with her rigid standards, her intolerance for ideas that didn't conform to her own, her expectation that he would take care of all of her household maintenance needs, her contempt for his wife and for the way they were raising their children. All he'd ever wanted was a family of his own, and in California, he finally had an opportunity to fully enjoy the one he had created.

However, something besides geographical distance had come between us at that point. I couldn't put my finger on it. We had always been able to pick up where we left off, able to catch up whenever the opportunity presented itself. We did hug each other and josh around together before the funeral service. But when I tried to get his email address in hopes that we would finally stay in touch, the one he gave me didn't work. When I called to get it again, he sounded distant and cross. And again the email address he gave didn't work.

A year later, Stephen dropped his kids off at school one morning and then pulled his car off the road. He called his wife to tell her he wasn't feeling well. He died there of a sudden, massive heart attack. He had no history of heart problems, had no warning. He was 51 years old.

Penny, Ed, Priscilla, Stephen; in Washington D.C., 1965

Penny

When our father died, Penny had just arrived in London for a three-year assignment as a civilian secretary with the Navy department. She'd been with the department in D.C. for a few years, hoping for an opportunity to travel; getting the London placement was a plum, perfect for visiting Europe and the Mediterranean. She seemed to be in her glory – a well-respected secretary, a world traveler, a grown daughter about whom her parents couldn't say enough. Priscilla and Ed talked about going to visit her in London, maybe doing a side trip to Scotland where their parents had been born.

Instead, Penny had to fly back for Dad's funeral, and fly back again for that first fatherless Christmas. She flew back for good at the end of the three-year assignment, with a passport full of stamps from her travels around the continent. "I've gone as high up in rank as I can as a civilian in the Navy Department," she said. "They're all telling me I could make a lot more money in the private sector."

Back in the states, jobless and at loose ends, she did what many young people of the early seventies were doing. She bought a car and went on a cross-country trip, starting in Washington, D.C., to see friends, then out to San Diego to see our cousin Lynn, heading back east through Scottsdale to see Lorraine. There, her life came to a complete stop. Unable to figure out where to go next, she stayed on and found herself dealing with the daily stresses of unemployment, poverty and taking care of Lorraine, whose health was deteriorating.

Penny and I had emerged from Marshall Road as plastic but workable replicas of sisters. We were cordial to each other, dutifully wrote to each other, called one another occasionally, remembered one another on birthdays and holidays. My first car was the one I bought from her when she went overseas. She sent me lighthearted photos and postcards from her travels. But her stay in Scottsdale changed that. She went from being the good girl admired for her many accomplishments to being stuck in the role of a social misfit: unemployed, living off the kindness of a relative, out of the mainstream.

Penny's life had been a dead end from the beginning. As the daughter who could do no wrong, she'd had to endure the torment of wondering, every day and all the time, if she would do something that displeased Priscilla and cause her mother to reverse our roles in the family. While she watched me being as good as gold and getting bullied, reviled and detested for it, she had to be feeling like an animal caught in a trap. How could she ever be herself, no matter how far away from Priscilla she lived?

When she was with Loraine, she became enraged by life in general, someone whose only way of coping with the road to nowhere was to snarl and hiss. She was increasingly unpleasant to Lorraine. Her manner towards me became Priscilla's manner; her voice became Priscilla's voice. Perhaps it was her only recourse: to become Priscilla, as she had been destined to become.

On a day when I had been eating macaroni for every meal for two weeks straight, thanks to gift coupons from the Welcome Wagon in the town where I had just taken a job, I sat in my one-bedroom basement apartment, a letter from Penny in my hand. Impoverished after a year-long master's degree program, I had sheets tacked over the windows because I couldn't yet afford curtains. Ironically, I had just opened an envelope from an anonymous neighbor, who had pointedly enclosed curtain ads from the local paper, which I also couldn't afford. Then I opened Penny's letter. "Now that you've gotten yourself a fancy job," Penny wrote from Scottsdale, "you need to be helping out around here! Think about others for a change! You ought to be able to start sending us money every month! Take some responsibility!"

After three years as Lorraine's caregiver, with Priscilla's financial help, Penny left Scottsdale, leaving Lorraine alone. "I just can't do it anymore," she said in a rare moment of sharing her feelings. "The only people I get to talk to are the ambulance guys who've come to take Lorraine to the hospital six times this past year." She started working full time with the same Connecticut firm that had been sending Lorraine freelance jobs she could do at home. Penny wrote to me that she needed medical care and massive amounts of dental work. I sent her money. She wrote that she used it for a toaster oven.

A year after her return to Connecticut, she called to tell me that Lorraine had died and not to bother flying out to Scottsdale because there wasn't going to be a service. She called back a few hour later to yell at me. "Did she send you her jade?" Lorraine's fabulous collection of jade carvings was missing, and Penny was convinced I had it. I didn't. But the tone of that phone call made me think that Penny's seemingly dutiful disposition of Lorraine's affairs was entirely mercenary. Those years of incessant poverty had left deep wounds; she was after whatever money she could gain.

Piece by piece, Penny put together a life modeled after what Lorraine's had been when we were kids. She lived close to Greenwich, got a condo and two cats, just like Lorraine. Using Lorraine's contacts, she started her own business, which, like Lorraine's, was a business that required cross-country travel. There was none of Lorraine's social life, or glamour, or joi de vivre, although Penny continued to take vacations abroad from time to time. As Lorraine had done for us, Penny played the role of a worldly and generous aunt to Stephen's children.

The friends she made in those days found her quiet and shy, a sweet girl who was emotionally reserved. She remained close to Priscilla, calling her two or three times a week and spending her holidays in Hingham every year. But with me, she continued to be hard-edged and cold, and the communication between us dwindled away to nothing. She stayed in touch with Auntie Belle, and I followed the events in Penny's life through Auntie Belle's conversations with me through the years.

When I, too, had a long spell of unemployment, resulting in a time when I was in debt to everyone I knew, I called Penny in desperation to ask for a loan. We had not spoken for years, but she reluctantly chatted for a while. I heard a heavy voice in that call, one that a stranger might have described as business-like and devoid of affect. I heard it as impatient, cross and depressed. But Penny's response to my financial predicament went above and beyond my expectations. She sent a check to cover all of my bills for that month. The next month, on her own initiative, she sent another check. And the next month as well. After that I was able to send her a note that I had finally landed a job and would repay her as soon as I could. She wrote back that I should put her at the bottom of the list of those I owed money to. And then she stopped communicating all together again. When I finally repaid her in full, years later, she never cashed the check.

I always believed that when our mother died, Penny and Stephen and I would find the time and the means to rebuild our relationship as siblings. In retrospect, I can see how much of my ongoing wishful thinking that reveals. For by the time Priscilla died, Penny had been in charge of our mother's affairs for years – paying Priscilla's bills, and paying herself generous amounts from our mother's checkbook. The old impoverishment still haunted her; she needed to know that she had money, that she could get more money if she needed it, that she had access to plenty of money.

One of her resources was the death of friends and relatives. She had not only handled Lorraine's will and estate, she had volunteered to do that for a few other people over the years. She offered to do it for our cousin Lynn when her mother was sick, and offered to do it for Auntie Belle. She knew her way around the probate system and the role of the executor of a will.

The year before Priscilla died, Penny convinced her to change her will. Penny had always been named as the executor, and Priscilla's will had always divided her property equally among we three kids. But a year before she died, based on whatever persuasive arguments Penny used over the years, true or false, Priscilla had her will rewritten to exclude me. Her lawyers got in touch with her immediately to let her know that change was alarming to them, not in her best interests, legally speaking, but she persisted. "The matter of Susan is not of concern at this time," she told them.

A few weeks after the funeral, on a weekend when Auntie Belle had mentioned to me that Penny was going to be at Priscilla's house, cleaning it up for sale, I called her there. I had carefully scripted a conversation I wanted to have with her, had it written down on a long sheet of yellow lined paper. "I want to come to Mum's house sometime before you sell it," I said.

"Why would you want to do that?" she asked.

"I want to see where she lived and how she lived in those last years. I think it would help me."

"I don't think being here would do anything," Penny said. "I've already gotten rid of a lot of stuff. There's nothing here to see."

"Still, I would like to come sometime."

"Why?"

"She was my mother," I said.

"Where were you when she had cancer?" Penny said, her voice as heavy as lead.

"Where were you when she was in the hospital for heart surgery and a pacemaker?"

"Where were you when she fainted and was all alone?"

"Where were you when she broke her foot?" She couldn't stop, just went on and on, getting louder and louder.

I could have responded in kind. "Where were you when I was being openly abused?"

"Where were you when I kept trying to establish some kind of relationship with her?"

But all I wanted to do is stop that verbal train wreck thundering toward me. I sat there and wrote down all that Penny was saying on my yellow pad, in shock at her diatribe but ever the cultivator of an accurate memory.

"I am not going to continue this conversation right now," I said finally, interrupting her. "I will call you back another time."

In my ignorance of what had transpired between Penny and Priscilla, as well as between Penny and Stephen, I waited to hear that the will had been probated. During the waiting, Penny sent Stephen and me a long letter about what she was doing with Priscilla's belongings, which arrived in large boxes that Penny had used to dutifully divide things up among we three kids: the china and silver, the knick knacks and linens, the stemware and serving dishes. Some of her notes were extremely thoughtful and touching.

"Do you remember these little glass nut baskets Mum used every Thanksgiving?"

"This platter originally belonged to Lorraine, so of course I thought you should have it, Susan."

After that awful phone call with Penny, I had written a letter to her asking if I could have something of our mother's that she had made, such as one of her crocheted afghans. Penny had included one of the beautiful white ones in my box. It was all grist for the mill of believing that now I would be included, now we three kids could have a relationship.

More months went by without notification that the will had been probated. Auntie Belle kept me posted on Penny's activities and let me know when Priscilla's house was sold. I finally called the Plymouth County Courthouse, and was told the will had been probated three months before. With a sinking feeling, I took a day off from work and drove for hours to get to the courthouse, where I fed a small fortune in coins into a copy machine and copied every page of documentation available on Priscilla's estate. While I was copying, I was trying hard not to read a word of it, to wait until I could go sit in the sun on the lawn across the street by the historic Plymouth harbor and take it all in. But I caught the most important phrase. "I have two children, Penny and Stephen." The shock was overwhelming.

I managed to get outside and sit by the water's edge, mere feet from Plymouth Rock, slowly reading every page, but my heart just kept breaking. Both Penny and Stephen had signed legal documentation that they were the only children of Priscilla. Not only had there been no resolution of my issues with Priscilla, but now it looked like there was no hope of any resolution with my siblings. How stupid I had been!

I understood why Stephen had seemed to discourage further contact between us after Priscilla's funeral. He and Penny had effectively buried the past and me along with it. They had also taken the money and run. Priscilla's estate was worth over $400,000.

I went back inside the courthouse and copied my father's will, just to read something that mentioned we three kids.

When the heartbreak wore off a little, the anger welled up. I sued Penny. She fought it, gave a deposition that rehashed all of my failures to act like a daughter to Priscilla. I wanted to let it go, did not want to suffer through a day in court hearing Penny orally describe all of the complaints Priscilla had had about my existence from the time I was born to the present, as if Penny were in court to be Priscilla. But the injustice was so great I couldn't let it go. I wanted her to know she had broken the law, wanted a judge to shame her for that.

After months of fruitless attempts to get a day in court, a series of calls came to me at work from my lawyer, who had caught up with Penny's lawyer long enough to promote some out-of-court negotiations. I was in the middle of a business conference and wanted desperately just to be done with it, so I caved in after the third call and agreed to the paltry settlement Penny's lawyers were offering. It was time to get on with my life.

In less than a year, Stephen would be dead. Within a couple of years, Penny sold her company, retired and moved to a condo in Florida, close to where Auntie Belle was living. An accomplished quilter, Penny joined a quilting group to take her craft to the next level. She contemplated the possibility of enrolling in college and getting a degree. But during her first year of retirement, Penny was diagnosed with Acute Myelogenous Leukemia, AML. Despite stem cell transplants and a firm conviction that she would beat this form of cancer, she died two years later at the age of 64.

When Auntie Belle had passed away the year before, Penny had driven over within the hour, ransacking Auntie Belle's home to look for cash she might have squirrelled away. She took pictures out of their frames, tore through closets and drawers, pulled everything out from under the beds. She found Auntie Belle's checkbook, and kept that to herself.

She found and destroyed the last will that Auntie Belle wrote, which divided her assets equally among Penny, Lynn and me, her last surviving relatives. Penny knew that there was an earlier version that she had helped Auntie Belle write, one that named Penny as an executor who could distribute Auntie Belle's money and belongings as she saw fit. That's the one she filed. Then she demanded a meeting with Auntie Belle's closest friends and insisted that they buy Belle's home directly from her, immediately.

During the last two years of her life, Penny had accrued a million and a half dollars in debt.

Susan, 2001

Susan

I am sixty-seven years old now, retired and deeply content with my life. I'm sure the angels have forgiven me for stealing songbooks when I was a kid. I used to sneak home a copy of whichever one we were using in school during an occasional "music period" so I could learn every single song inside. Sitting on the edge of my bed, Lorraine's bed, I'd read music and memorize verses until I could sing each song in my head without making a sound. Thousands of them are stored in my memory, any one of which is apt to burst out in a moment of happiness. This morning it was, "Winter's a comin'. The geese are getting fat. Please put a feather in the old man's hat!"

By the time I graduated from high school, I was 5'7" tall and weighed 95 pounds. My arms stuck out from the sleeves of dresses like little sticks. My eyes were rimmed with dark circles, sunken back into their bony sockets. I had been getting sick to my stomach during the night, almost every night, for two years. I couldn't have survived Priscilla for much longer, but surviving her did not bring immediate relief. The physical and emotional conditions resulting from her abuse took twice as long to fade as they had taken to develop. That kind of stress unwinds exceedingly slowly. I don't think it completely unwound until Penny's death, until the last member of my immediate family was no longer on this earth.

Looking back on all those years of recovery, I can see now how I used relationships and life experiences to help meet the enduring need for mothering. From an early age, music was my soul mate. As a child, it could soothe me, calm me, put me to sleep – just like a mother. I could disappear from that motherless house into worlds of comfort or joy or love or courage. "Just what makes a little ole ant think he'll move that rubber tree plant? Anyone knows an ant can't move a rubber tree plant. But he has high hopes, he has high hopes . ." (J. Van Heusen and S. Cahn, 1959). I was that ant. I was also Scheherazade trying to stay alive for a thousand more nights, and Anna whistling a happy tune in the King and I. Once free of Priscilla, I consumed music the way the hungry consume a nutritious meal. The need for music – from pop to classical, from musical theater to opera – was fierce and nearly as physical as an addiction.

Getting degrees in education turned out to be a fortunate source of comfort and courage as well. I was required to read about child development, adolescent development, psychology, parenting, abnormalities, moral and cognitive reasoning, family relationships, communication skills and a host of other topics professional educators delve into in order to become teachers and professors. My colleagues were wise and caring role models. The field of education was a surrogate mother, teaching me many things about normalcy I had been unable to learn through family experience. It helped me to discover parts of myself that were thriving despite my past, and parts that needed recovery. I found support and resources in the field of education for my continued growth and development, and a lot of guidance on becoming a more fully mature person as well as a good teacher.

I lived alone. That was how I was used to functioning. Having time alone helped me to contemplate each day's events, in order to understand this novel world of ordinary human interaction. Living with Priscilla taught me to consider everything I did carefully and logically, from multiple angles. Even though the years of daily tyranny were finally behind me, the habit of scrutinizing my behavior continued. I needed to ensure that each act, each moment, was carried out in the best way possible, including uttering my thoughts and expressing my feelings.

At the same time, I discovered that the world is full of mothering people! Anyone who was kind and caring felt like a mother to me, and I met people like that everywhere. Professors, students, colleagues, friends, supervisors: everyone had this natural warmth that was so striking to me. They all seemed to think I had something to offer. Come to find out, in the real world people give you their affection and attention freely, all the time, even when you barely know them! It was overwhelming.

For a while, I fell in love with just about everyone in my life. If someone liked me a little bit, I was hopelessly smitten.

Supervisors seemed to be easily impressed, compared to Priscilla. Although I felt like I was doing what was expected, my supervisors and colleagues always made me feel that I had something extra, as if I was somehow special. The more they remarked on my skills, the more I leaned on my intellect, dug into my teaching jobs and worked long hours. I felt like I was reaping lavish praise for things that came naturally.

Of course I wanted to succeed at something! I'd waited my whole life for that experience, and when my profession started giving me positive feedback, I gave back in spades, piling on more and more credentials and leadership responsibilities until the mental and physical wellsprings ran dry. Every five years or so, I experienced a period of professional burn out, requiring a breather and a fresh start.

During one of those transitions, I came back to Massachusetts to get my Doctorate at the University. I was in my early thirties, and had begun to think about re-establishing relationships with my aunts and uncles. The university is located a couple of hours away from Boston in the western part of the state, but it was close enough to arrange visits with the relatives during academic breaks. They were all of retirement age with time available.

For some time I had been wishing I could probe the memories of these people who had been closest to our family to see what they had thought of my childhood. I hoped they could shed light on the origins of my relationship with Priscilla, who had so vehemently shut the door on any further communication between us. Visiting the aunts and uncles was the first of my small rebellions, a self-determined act of trying to make a family for myself out of the pieces that remained, beyond Priscilla's reach. I also secretly hoped that when they ran into Priscilla at the mall or had dinner with her over the holidays, they'd let it slip that they'd seen me, and tell her how wonderful I was.

To a person, the aunts and uncles welcomed me with open arms. More importantly, they couldn't wait to talk to Susan the adult about how they had suffered through my childhood. I had not anticipated this part of the process. They had been waiting for this moment, eager to tell me how awful they felt about witnessing time after time Priscilla's overt animosity towards me. I didn't have to search for the right way to raise the subject in order to probe their memories. They talked openly of their frustrations at being powerless to help. Uncle Ralph wept each time we talked. They all wanted my understanding and my forgiveness.

Over the course of the next five years, we talked and talked. We had weekend visits and spent holidays together. They gave me stacks of family photographs that no longer held much meaning for them; I saw pictures of myself as an infant and toddler for the first time, and cherished them as if they restored that missing phase of my life. I listened to my elders tell colorful and unedited stories about the many Scottish émigrés in the family and their own childhoods. They gave me the sense of family history I had been lacking. As they shared remembrances of my mother and father as children and as a young married couple, they speculated about Grammie's influence on Priscilla, and expressed great frustration at the way Dad's religious beliefs thwarted their longing to rescue me from harm. But we could not solve Priscilla. We could get angry and sorrowful about the past, we could share hitherto unshared anecdotes, but we could not figure out what drove Priscilla to such lengths.

"She was like that even as a little kid," Uncle Bud said, "stomping her foot if people didn't agree with her. She couldn't stand it if your ideas were different. You had to think the way she thought."

"It was because you didn't look like her people," Uncle Ralph said. "You looked like your father's people."

"I suppose it was that middle child thing," Auntie Belle said.

"It was because you were lively!" Aunt Wilma said. "The other two you could plunk down anywhere and they'd just sit there like a blob, but you were full of life!"

One Christmas during this time I joined Uncle Ralph and his family for the weekend. As we got ready for church on Christmas morning, a car pulled into his driveway.

Time After Time

"That's your mother's car," Uncle Ralph said. "I wonder what she's doing here? We haven't seen her for about five years!"

"I'm going to go in the bedroom and shut the door," I said, my consternation at Priscilla's sudden appearance causing me to revert immediately into the role of the banished child. "It will be a bad scene if she sees me here, so I'll just stay away until she's gone."

"No way!" said Uncle Ralph. "You'll stay right out here with us!" He went to the front door to greet her as she rang the bell.

"What a surprise! Merry Christmas, Pete," he said to her, giving her a hug.

"Merry Christmas," she said, grinning up at him.

"We were just getting ready to go to church," he said. "Would you like to come with us?"

"Oh, no," Priscilla said. "I'm on my way to Bud's for dinner and just thought I'd stop by to give you this. I can't stay long." She handed him a gaily wrapped package with a big silver bow on it.

"Come on in," Uncle Ralph said, taking her coat and leading her to the living room.

I hadn't seen her for ten years and still got that electric body ripple of fierce longing and primal fear in her presence, so I stood on wobbly legs in the door of the kitchen with a stupid grin on my face. "Merry Christmas," I said as she passed by. My heart was racing.

She peered at me, "Oh. You must be Karen." That was the name of my cousin's fiancé.

Ralph gave a little snort. "No," he said. "That's your daughter Susan."

Priscilla snapped her hand in front of her face as if to swat me away, said not a word, and sat awkwardly in the living room while my uncle and aunt opened her gift – a silly little teapot – and tried to manufacture polite conversation. My cousins, one newly engaged the other married, spoke to their Auntie Pete warmly and chatted about the things they were up to while I sat in the chair farthest away from her. But talk about an elephant in the room! Priscilla's face had settled into that frozen mask of hatred I remembered so well. After five minutes, she got up to leave.

"Aren't you going to wish your daughter Merry Christmas?" Uncle Ralph said as he helped her on with her coat.

"Oh. Why should I," she said with another dismissive flip of her hand, and left.

Life went on. The world is full of loving women who are as gifted at nurturing friends as they are at nurturing their young. I found these women wherever I went, or we found each other. For all of my own child-bearing years, I was Aunt Sue to the children my friends were having, becoming a close member of the family to one family after another, decade after decade. For I was a nurturer, too, with a career in early childhood education and a knack for perceiving what individual children as well as stressed out mothers needed from the adults around them. These relationships were a primary source of emotional and spiritual balance for the intellectual skills I relied on so heavily.

But after I got my doctorate, I started sliding into depression. I couldn't find a job, stopped playing guitar and singing with friends, avoided opportunities to paste myself onto others' families, had to get roommates to help pay the bills, developed unrealistic expectations about becoming a writer and floundered around, unable to articulate any practical plans for what I was going to do with my life. I gained more and more weight, drank more and more wine. When I finally landed a job and started to get back on my feet professionally and financially, I felt like a failure – a dysfunctional, overweight, almost middle-aged woman who could not achieve a damn thing she wanted. No marriage, no children, no writing career, no social life, no way to continue living in the geographical area I loved, where I had felt a sense of belonging since the day I arrived at the University. Instead, economic necessity was forcing me to move back to New Hampshire and take yet another job in education – the two things I had longed to avoid.

It was to be the final phase of my academic career. The cocoons I had woven out of solitude and professional accomplishment had begun to unravel. It was time to figure out what would make me a happy person. Although I continued the old patterns of burying myself in work, tacking myself onto a family with young children and living alone, I began to take the craft of writing seriously. I wrote on weekends and vacations and started submitting my work to newspapers and magazines. The process of writing made me feel whole, fully satisfied with who I was and what my capabilities were.

Along the way I had my ears pierced. It was a token gesture, deliberately doing something that would definitely not please my mother. I assumed I'd never see her again anyway. A year later, after a great deal of thought, I went to court to change my name. My academic position required daily interactions with dozens of people – few of whom could spell or pronounce Dalziel. Hearing the name over and over, seeing the name, correcting people on the pronunciation and spelling of the name was a constant reminder of my history. It was time to move on. Anderson had been Lorraine's maiden name, and that was the name I chose, to honor her.

"I don't understand why you changed your name," Auntie Belle said, puzzled. "Your father was such a good man."

I knew the grapevine would get word of this unconscionable act back to Priscilla, knew it was futile to try and mute the aftershocks, but I gave it a shot. "I thought so, too," I said to Auntie Belle. "He was. That's why I kept his name as a middle name."

To close friends I said, "I'm divorcing my family. I don't know how else to put it. I have got to start making a life for myself that's different from the life I've been living, and I don't think I can do that if I'm still Susan Dalziel."

Shortly afterward, Uncle Bud died. I suffered through Priscilla's ostracism at the wake and at the funeral, where she hemmed herself in between Penny and Auntie Belle, where the receiving line left no room for me to seat myself among the other nieces and nephews, where I sat like a stranger in the crowd, unacknowledged by my mother, my sister, my brother. I watched Priscilla stroke Penny's hand rhythmically as they sat together. Two peas in a pod the way Grammie and Priscilla had been two peas in a pod. I watched Penny get up and go to the guest book to note that I had signed in with my new name, then look over at me coldly. I went through the receiving line as if I was just a face in the crowd, furious at being relegated to that role when I had been so close to Uncle Bud during the past few years. My mother turned her back and marched away when I approached. "Have you met Mum's boss?" Penny said sweetly, as if we had been chatting like sisters all day, turning me towards a stranger and introducing me.

When I got to where my brother was in the line, he remained seated and whispered, "So don't be such a stranger, hmmm?" I laughed out loud, because the whole scene was so bizarre.

Back at Uncle Bud's solidly built house with the gorgeous view of the Taunton River, I wedged myself and my pierced ears between cousin Lynn and cousin Donnie on the couch, where I sat smoking and drinking companionably with them in full view of Priscilla. Susan the rebel rises again. How Priscilla glared at me!! She turned her whole body towards me as she sat with the aunts at Uncle Bud's dining table, and gave me a good, long glare. I got up and got another drink, had another cigarette.

But the entire event was so upsetting, I finally sought therapy. I was nearly 40 years old, still gaining weight, still traumatized in so many ways despite years of reading and talking to friends and growing up and earning professional respect and trying my best on my own to overcome my past. Putting myself in the hands of a gifted and talented therapist was an important step. Priscilla remained an unsolvable enigma, but two years of therapy began to give some shape to my sense of self, the individual who lived apart from Priscilla. Finally I started looking forward instead of backward, not knowing that I had entered a complex, ten-year process of salvaging what was left of my life.

One cold, spring weekend I went to Martha's Vineyard for a solitude, huddling in the dunes and listening to the ocean. It was inevitable that I would decide to leave my secure academic position. In order to be myself, be authentic, I felt I needed to completely strip myself of the professional roles I'd been playing and give myself completely to the writing life. The only issue was finding the courage to do it. I returned home with a date in mind and started the process of disentangling myself from that which was strangling me.

Time After Time

Just when submitting my resignation looked like the stupidest thing I could have done, when I was days away from filing for unemployment, when my belongings were packed up and in storage and I had no idea where I was going to live or how I was going to pay rent, I was offered an opportunity to ghost write a book for friends, who happened to own a vacation home on an island off the coast of Maine. They couldn't pay me as a writer, but they offered to let me live in the island house while we were working on the book.

I spent two years of utter isolation in that spot, on the edge of the wilderness, feeling like pioneer woman even though the house was modern and tight and the wood pile enormous. I wrote every day, mastered my first computer, read volumes and volumes about the craft of writing and submitted articles and book proposals for my own work as well as the ghost writing project. Surrounded by the mighty tide that ebbed and flowed against the rocky shore just ten feet from the house, jittery from hundreds of unfamiliar sounds my hyper-vigilant ears had to learn to identify, I endured brutal weather and made constant adjustments to the difficulties of living alone on an island.

When it was over, friends asked, "Did that experience change you?"

"Oh, yes," I said. "I'm tougher now."

But it takes a while for the real effects of such a dramatic solitude to emerge from the deep recesses of the soul. The molting process was underway, but far from over. I continued living alone until I was 50, although I moved back to western Massachusetts, determined to root myself in the geographical area I loved. I turned my back on the field of education and began taking low-paying jobs in the business world, part-time jobs that allowed me to continue writing during the day. Economically, it was a disaster, but it did get better. Over time, I worked my way up to full time management and leadership positions, most of which involved a great deal of writing.

When I met a woman my age at work who was still trying to make peace with her own upbringing, who was divorced and struggling with getting her bearings, I began to realize that I was ready to give up my insistence on living alone and join forces with another human being, especially one who could appreciate an unconventional family history. As we began to do things together, we talked about looking for an apartment to share. That's what the island experience did for me. I helped me to realize that there is a difference between enjoying time alone and choosing to live a life alone. I was ready to give up living a life alone.

We have since bought a house together, and made ourselves into a semblance of family for each other. We have birthday traditions and holiday traditions, neighbors and friends, people we call our tribe. The house is situated across the street from the Connecticut River, with a small mountain in back. The surroundings fill us with joy and contentment. We are learning how to give up a little of that fierce independence we both cultivated for so long, learning how to trade it in for some healthy forms of inter-dependence. I have become a decent cook, and a bit of a foodie. An avid gardener as well, I've dug up huge amounts of our half-acre yard, by hand, with a pitchfork. I've planted perennials everywhere and photographed flowers by the hundreds. Now that I am retired, I write every day.

But three o'clock in the afternoon rolls around every day and starts gnawing at something inside. It's the old anticipatory anxiety, the hour of walking home from school every day, the moment of facing Priscilla and the life I lived at home. That life is long gone now, but the muscles and nerves have their own indelible memory that cannot be transformed by all the contentment in the world. Every day I plan ways of keeping busy in the late afternoons.

When Penny died, a friend of hers mailed to me some boxes of her personal effects, including a lot of family papers and photographs. I have Mum's last driver's license, the diplomas of both parents, my sister's passport, the annual school photos of my brother's children and every single one of Penny's school report cards. There is an old letter from Dad to Penny, with his advice on romance. I have more photos of myself, in pictures taken of we three kids at the beach, in the back yard, gathered around the fireplace with the cousins one Christmas on Marshall Road. The box also contained a treasure beyond words.

While Penny was cleaning out Priscilla's house, she had come across and saved a collection of letters Dad and Mum had written to each other over a two-week period. His company sent him to a training session at the IBM institute in Edicott, NY, a campus where he lived in a dorm, ate in a dining hall with other participants from around the country and attended daily classes in various IBM office machines and business procedures. It was February, 1946, the tail end of a harsh winter. Penny had just turned three years old. I was eight months old. My parents wrote to each other every day during those two weeks, sending their letters air mail so that they would arrive in a day or two.

Priscilla's letters are full of humor and affection, despite the burdens of temporarily being a single parent to two very small girls. She writes of her daily household chores, her cooking and shopping, and her interactions with family, neighbors and friends. Our neighbor Ruthie's husband Charlie was still in the service at that time, so Priscilla had arranged for Ruthie to stay with her during those two weeks to help out with the girls while Ed was away. Ruthie went to work every day, but had breakfast and dinner with Priscilla; the two of them spent their evenings writing letters to their husbands, washing each other's hair, mending clothes, gabbing away and listening to comedy shows on the radio. Together they dealt with cranky children, a plugged sink, a broken furnace and a lot of snowfall.

Each letter also has an anecdote or two about the antics of the children. These were a surprise.

February 19:
"Susan finally has a tooth! Really this time! Gee she was cute with the photographer yesterday! You know how she bounces when you go in to take her out of the crib? Well, he arranged a couple of pillows across the front of the big chair and had her lying on her tummy facing the camera. Everything was fine until he got ready to snap the picture, and every single time, she started to bounce! He thought she was wonderful! We'll see the results next week."

February 20:
"Susan's been _so_ good, Dear. Even changing didies and dressing doesn't bother her. It's wonderful!! She's so darn cute, honey, I wish you could have her with you."

February 23:
"I put Pen and Sue out while I washed floors, so they had almost an hour outside. It's a beautiful day today, very warm and springy. The

first tiny point of another of Sue's teeth is poking through today, so she should have two full-grown ones when you get home. She grows sweeter and dearer every day, sweetheart."

February 25:
"If you see Aunt Jessie and Uncle Willie, please give them my very best, and tell them I hope we'll see them soon, because we've got a new little package they'd love! Gee, she's cunnin', dear!"

So this is where the story ends. Once upon a time, my mother loved me.

About The Author

Susan D. Anderson earned her doctorate in Instructional Leadership at the University of Massachusetts in 1980 and had a distinguished career in early childhood education and teacher education. During those years in academia, writing became her primary interest, along with a desire to tell the extraordinary story of her own childhood. She began work on this memoir during two years spent in solitude on a tiny island off the coast of Maine. After a second career as a writer and manager in educational corporations, Susan retired in order to write full time. An accumulation of her signature "essays for the soul" can be found on her web site, www.sunderlassieexpress.com. Susan lives in the Connecticut River valley of western Massachusetts, where she is content to write, cook, garden and take photographs of her flowers. *Time After Time* is her first book.